£8-50

James Ward R.A.
Animal Painter 1769–1859
and his England

Also by G. E. Fussell

Chronological list of early agricultural works in the library of the Ministry of Agriculture. *H.M.S.O.* 1930.

The exploration of England: a select bibliography of travel and topography, 1570–1815. *Mitre Press.* 1935.

Robert Loder. Farm accounts 1610–1620. ed. for *Royal Hist. Soc. Camden Soc.* 3rd ser. v. 53. 1936.

Farming systems from Elizabethan to Victorian days in the north and east ridings of Yorkshire. *York. Castle Museum.* 1944.

The old English farming books from Fitzherbert to Tull, 1523–1730. *Crosby Lockwood.* 1947.

Village life in the 18th century. *Littlebury, Worcester.* 1947.

From Tolpuddle to T.U.C.: a century of farm labourers' politics. *Windsor Press, Slough.* 1948.

Sir Hugh Plat. Delightes for Ladies; with introductions by G. E. & K. R. Fussell. *Crosby Lockwood.* 1948.

The English rural labourer; his home, furniture, clothing & food from Tudor to Victorian times. *Batchworth Press.* 1949.

More old English farming books; from Tull to the Board of Agriculture, 1731–1793. *Crosby Lockwood.* 1950.

The farmers' tools, 1500–1900; the history of British farm implements tools and machinery before the tractor came. *Andrew Melrose.* 1952.
with K. R. Fussell. The English countrywoman, a farmhouse social history A.D. 1500–1900. *Melrose.* 1953.

with K. R. Fussell. The English Countryman, his life and work, A.D. 1500–1900. *Melrose* 1955.

Agriculture; techniques of farming in Singer, Chas & ors. eds. A history of technology. v. 4. *Clarendon Press.* 1958.

Growth of food production in idem. v. 5. 1958.

Ernle. (R. E. Prothero) English farming past & present. new ed. (6th) with introductions by G. E. Fussell & O. R. McGregor. *Heinemann.* 1961.

The English dairy farmer, 1500–1900. *Frank Cass.* 1966.

Farming technique from prehistoric to modern times. *Pergamon Press.* 1966.

The story of farming. *Pergamon Press.* 1969.

Crop nutrition: science and practice before Liebig. *Coronado Press, Box 3232, Lawrence, Kansas 66044.*

The Classical Tradition in West European Farming. *David & Charles.* 1972.

Jethro Tull; his influence on mechanised agriculture. *Osprey Publishing. Reading.* 1973.

Frontispiece James Ward as a young man

James Ward R.A.

Animal Painter 1769-1859 and his England

G. E. FUSSELL

London
MICHAEL JOSEPH

First published in Great Britain by Michael Joseph Ltd
52 Bedford Square, London WC1
1974

© 1974 G. E. Fussell

ISBN 0 7181 1242 3

Printed in Great Britain by
Butler & Tanner Ltd, Frome and London
and bound by
Dorstel Press, Harlow

Contents

Illustrations

Author's Introduction

No claim is made to anything strikingly original here, and anyone who is looking for lightning strokes of glittering verbiage may as well abandon the book for there is little original that can be said about this overworked period. The incidents and changes of the time have been described so often as almost to make this book superfluous were it not for the striking character of the central figure, and the part he played in the artistic life of his day, a part that was played in very varying circumstances during a period of formidable changes in the life of numbers of the English people of all degrees, degrees which were indeed more marked and more effectively imposed and underlined than in modern times. The way of life and environment of the curtly and effectively defined classes was nevertheless affected profoundly by the economic and technical changes at work during the three or more generations of Ward's long life, ninety years from 1769 to 1859.

James Ward was a short, thickset man, and like most men of his physical type (not excepting most others) he thought no small beer of himself, and developed this characteristic of greatness to an exceedingly unnecessary degree. His talent as a painter and engraver was outstanding, but possibly not so great as his own estimate of it. He was, like Dickens, born in very humble circumstances, and it was by chance that he was able to remove himself to a higher sphere just in the way that chance plays so large a part in most people's lives.

Ward was born nine years after George III came to the throne. The year 1760 was formerly given great significance as the beginning of the so-called industrial revolution, but this climacteric

is now relegated to the shadows of the most elementary text-
books. Long before that date an agricultural revolution was
incubating. It closely affected the animals that Ward was to paint.
The new crops that were to transform arable farming and to
provide winter fodder for the livestock had long been introduced,
and were spreading over the countryside as more and more
farmers became convinced of their profitable value. Most particularly these new fodder crops that kept the parents in heart
during the winter were important to their offspring, who were
perhaps the ancestors of the animals that Ward was commissioned to paint the portraits of.

The appearance of the landscape too was being changed, as it
had more slowly been changed in the past. Enclosure of open field
and waste had been going on slowly and sporadically for centuries. The rate at which this work was done increased with speed
in the late eighteenth century. Before its end thousands of acres
had been transmogrified, and the new 'quick' hedges around
the enclosed fields gave a pleasant picturesqueness to the flourishing farming, of tenants and landowners alike.

The majority of English people then were rural people, but
the great industrial cities were to be built during Ward's lifetime,
and when he died their population was much the larger proportion of the English people. In the meantime the landed interest,
the noblemen and country gentlemen, ruled a nation mostly of
farmers and their men. Though they still played a major part in
the country's affairs at the end of Ward's life, the industrial
interest had already secured the repeal of the Corn Laws before
his death, no small sign of the changes already made and to come.

It was this rural scene, its pleasures, its horses, cattle, sheep
and pigs that James Ward was to paint and engrave for nearly a
century. But his brother William had forestalled him in the
artistic profession. James was always a little jealous of William
(for this and other reasons). He, James, had less education than
William because of his father's self-inflicted financial losses: so
he started work in what he rightly thought was a more humble
capacity, and was only retrieved from this degradation by his

brother's efforts. The consequence was that James felt frustrated and created within himself what we might call an inferiority complex. He became shockingly antagonistic and truculent in his personal relations. He often saw offence where none could have been intended, was more than brusque to his patrons, and extraordinarily tyrannical towards his children. He guided his life by a most austere religion, and he worked like a demon.

His output was tremendous and he earned a great deal of money, but he despised the work that brought it in. He wanted to shine in a somewhat outmoded fashion, and his Waterloo *Allegory* was a disaster. He was unwilling to accept the limitations of his gifts, and his struggles to make himself into something he was not were heartbreaking and naturally unsuccessful but in spite of this idiosyncrasy during the whole of his life he continued to paint and engrave the rural scene, country people and their occupations, their amusements and their prize animals.

Talented men have a habit of thwarting the development of their gifts by refusing to accept the limitations of what may, for want of a better word, be described as their gifts. James Ward was one of these. He wanted to be something different from what he was (who doesn't) because he had mistaken ideas about the circumstances of his time, a decade less than a century, in which he lived. It is true that there was still at the end of the eighteenth century a taste for the heroic and historical subject by the buyers of individual paintings, but there was an expanding market amongst the middle class that was becoming more numerous and more wealthy for engravings made from paintings of simple rural scenes and rustic life. These people were well-to-do but not so rich as the landed aristocracy who ruled, and may be said to have owned the country.

Ward lived through almost a century, most significant in the history of the England he loved so well and depicted so delightfully. These are two excellent reasons, or so they seem, for writing a book about James Ward and the England in which he lived, the events he must have seen, the people he met, and the pictures he painted and engraved. It was an England that has

now vanished into limbo, but not it may be hoped, of forgotten things. Ward and his compeers suffice to remind a later
generation of what its ancestors did and how they lived.

                                                        G.E.F.

A Note on James Ward's Paintings

Possibly because he was so curiously variable, both in the quality and kind of art he produced, James Ward remains a rather neglected figure, quite diminished by a number of more substantial reputations in the great romantic era of English painting. Yet it is in that direction, looking towards the essentially modern in artistic developments, that his most striking achievement is to be discovered; not (as has been too frequently suggested) as the obvious successor to Morland, perpetuating an already trivialised version of the sentimental pastoral, and certainly not as the vain rhetorician of another outdated school, contending still with grandiose historical themes in a manner based, quite without taste or conviction, on a faded recollection of High Art and the Baroque; nor is it even his altogether more appealing activity in that field wherein he strove uniquely among English artists, to record without hint of anecdotic interest a direct and sturdy portrayal of animate nature, with hogs that are simply hoggish, and in artistic tradition, more French than English. It is on the other hand – and this is surely a complexity of the artist born of a momentous epoch – in the very reversal of that last mood, and in a deeply subjective and emotional apprehension of the wild and fearful in nature, that his vision most surely compels the modern spectator; the savagery of the *Boa Serpent*, like some Fuseli nightmare become real, and the sublime power of that dark void within *Gordale Scar*, are typical, and perhaps insufficiently acknowledged, portents of expressionism in modern art.

ALAN TOMPKINS

CHAPTER I

Childhood in London

A child born in London in the middle of the eighteenth century was fortunate if he survived the perils of birth, and luckier still to live to maturity. The deeper in the heart of the city, the greater the dangers. Overcrowding was rife, and the streets were filthy with animal and household refuse, more so where the population was densest; possibly less so in the districts where the wealthy lived.

James Ward was born in Thames Street in 1769. It was a particularly unsavoury neighbourhood. It was not much better when I worked there about 1909, 140 years later, but must have been much worse in 1769. The beaches of the river at low tide then were the happy hunting ground of the mudlark, and the playground of the children of the neighbourhood. On Dowgate Hill there was a great dunghill, a collecting and shipping point for the stable manure of the town, and of the innumerable indoor dairies whence a large part of the daily milk supply was obtained. (Hundreds of tons of animal refuse had to be cleared from the innumerable stables daily.)

'The lily of Malud', sang Sir John Squire, 'it blossometh in mud', so paraphrasing a common saying of our grandmothers. They justified letting the children make mud pies by proclaiming that the sweetest flowers grew in dirt. A flower of genius was nourished in the ill-flavoured locality of Thames Street in the 1770's. James Ward spent his childhood there.

All his life long he loathed the idea that he had been born in that place. Nearly eighty years later, after a famous and distinguished career, during which he had travelled over the greater part of the country upon profitable commissions or pleasurable visits, and had mingled with the great and fashionable, Ward retained vivid memories of the squalid conditions of his early life. These memories haunted him with an intensity of feeling only to be compared with Dickens' shuddering recollections of his youthful employment in a blacking factory. In his old age Ward comforted himself with the reflection that his family had been better off before he was born, the truth of this being demonstrated by his elder brother William's education at Merchant Taylors school. This left a permanent and indelible feeling of grievance in James' mind. Still nursing his sense of injury nearly seventy years later he wrote to his son George, in a letter dated 28th Dec. 1847, 'My mother became destitute about the time of my birth. My brother being 7 years older than myself had a very good education at the Merchant Taylors School upon Dowgate Hill. . . Instead of having the benefit of the School, before I could read or write (but as I would judge it out) my Father took me into the Cellar.' In that cellar he was set to washing out cider bottles and such like menial tasks.

The city, his natal place, the largest and most populous in the country, was small if compared with the gigantic sprawl of modern London. Its half a million inhabitants lived in severely overcrowded conditions, and this stimulated building, so that the town was growing fairly rapidly. Much of the building followed the line of the roads, a ribbon development two centuries old. In the west the rich moved away from Covent Garden, Soho Square and St. Giles to new streets built around Cavendish Square, Hanover Square, Grosvenor Square and New Bond Street. The streets west of Haymarket and towards St. James's had been built in the previous century, as had Greek Street, and some streets on the west of Tottenham Court Road. The east of the town too, was filling up; Shoreditch and Whitechapel, and the area south of the river was being 'developed'.

Farm land adjoined Great Russell Street, and on clear days the heights of Highgate and Hampstead could be seen. The new road from Paddington to Islington provided another opportunity for the speculative builder. Much of its length comprised Marylebone Road, Euston Road and Pentonville Road, where some houses built in the eighteenth century are still standing, though many have been swept away to make place for blocks of modern flats. South of the river buildings began to appear from Westminster to Southwark. Stepney and Hackney had ceased to be country retreats, and become strongholds of overcrowding and poverty.

Much of this building was shoddy, but it demanded bricks and the kilns providing them were spread round the town, and were one cause of disgust to sensitive people. The activities on the edges of London rendered them displeasing to both sight and smell. A poetaster writing a few years after Ward's birth says:—

> Where'er around I cast my Wand'ring eyes,
> Long rows of fetid bricks arise,
> And nauseous dunghills smell in mouldering heaps,
> While the fat sow beneath the covert sleeps.
> I spy no verdant glade, no gushing rill,
> No fountain gushing from the rocky hill,
> But stagnant pools adorn our dusty plains,
> Where half-starved cows wash down their meal of grains.

London's country of those days was not very savoury, particularly that part of it accessible to people walking, riding horseback, perhaps like John Gilpin, or in a horse-drawn vehicle. The roads passed between land cut up by drains, open to the air, laystalls and heaps of garbage. Pigs, as the poet said, were kept near the town, and fed on its 'kitchen waste'. 'Graziers, cowkeepers, hog-keepers, brickmakers, scavengers, nightmen, nursery and market gardeners alike monopolised most of the land round London.' Open spaces like Lincoln's Inn Fields, and Tothill Fields in Westminster, were used as town dumps for all sorts of rubbish, and must have smelt to high heaven. Over these dumps half-wild pigs rambled, competing with miserable, starving specimens of human beings for the rancid bread and stinking meat cast there.

Our ancestors had no very sensitive noses, though there were many amongst them who preached improvement. These conditions remained well into the nineteenth century despite reformers.

Important amongst the changes gradually being wrought
when Ward was a boy, was the building of Westminster Bridge,
and later Blackfriars Bridge, an undertaking praised by Smollet
in *Humphrey Clinker*. The foul-smelling Fleet River had been
covered in from Fleet Street to Holborn, and squares like Lincoln's Inn Fields were being fenced to keep away the rogues and
vagabonds who sojourned in their uncared-for wastes.

Nothing is known of the home of the Wards in Thames Street
because James gives no details, but it can have been no different
from others under the prevailing conditions. House room was
scarce all over the city and almost every building was overcrowded.
A cellar or garret was a tenement for a family, the former often
being business premises as well as dwelling house. It is common
form of romantic literature to describe an aspirant to literary
distinction spending his struggling years in a garret. Nothing
could have been more painfully accurate of Ward's London.
Between the cellar and the garret each room might be occupied
by a family, where parents and children slept, and the man carried on his trade. Many of these family rooms, too, were let
furnished, often on a week to week basis. Was it in such a room
that Ward's father, the foreman of a fruit and cider dealer,
brought up his family; or was he one of the more fortunate who
rented a couple of rooms. A good deal of this crowded living was
the result of centuries-old usage, and some other part of the
necessity for a man to live close to his work at whatever cost in
comfort, when his only transport was shank's mare.

In such conditions personal or domestic cleanliness, in our
sense of the term, was both impossible and unknown. Sheets, if
there were any, might be washed as much as three times a year.
Even where no sheets were used blankets and coverlets were
never washed, or were renewed only when 'no longer tenable'.
Curtains hung unwashed until they fell to pieces. They helped to
darken rooms already dark enough from the huddle of surrounding buildings. Streets and houses were full of a foetid, leaden
and oppressive air.

Clothing was not even designed for washing. The wives of
journeymen, tradesmen, and shopkeepers, the class to which

Ward's father belonged, wore leather stays that were never washed though worn daily for years. Tradesmen's wives and even gentlewomen wore petticoats of camblet, lined with dyed linen, stuffed with wool and horsehair and quilted, 'day by day until they were rotten'. One of the great benefits of the industrial change that took place in the last part of the eighteenth century was the production of cheap cotton goods. Cotton dresses and other garments were not so expensive as those formerly worn, and it was necessary to wash them, so personal cleanliness 'followed' almost as a matter of course.

Such personal and domestic living generously disseminated disease. Typhus was endemic, as was 'fever', things almost unknown today. What was worse, medical attention was almost exclusively the prerogative of the well-to-do. Little was known or cared about the health of the poor who lived in such a crowded and disastrous situation. The foundation of the first dispensary, in the same year as Ward was born, was possibly more important than the setting up of the Royal Academy in that year. It was situated in Red Lion Square, and directed by a Dr. Armstrong, who hoped to treat the children of the lower classes. Their parents had a confirmed opinion that it was useless to call a doctor to them because they could not describe their ailments. They were killed or cured by the nostrums of old wives or quacks. It was not until the end of the century that 'fever' cases were isolated. Before that sufferers were taken to hospital in public conveyances and were put to bed amongst other patients, so that both hospitals and workhouses were ravaged by this and other infectious diseases. When a home was vacated by death from this cause, it was not disinfected, and was speedily reoccupied by some other family who were very likely just as speedily infected. The conditions were only changed late in the century when arrangements were made for infected premises to be whitewashed and cleansed.

The water supply, too, was badly contaminated in spite of the construction of the New River in the reign of James I. Smollet makes Matthew Bramble, the irascible, kindly Welsh squire, who became the patron of *Humphrey Clinker*, say of London 'If I would drink water, I must quaff the maukish contents of an open acqueduct exposed to all manner of defilement or swallow that which comes from the river Thames, impregnated with all the filth of London and Westminster.'

Over-indulgence in alcohol, one of the social habits of the time, was inexpressibly costly in human life, both directly and indirectly. Few of our ancestors were noteworthy for sobriety, though many people in town and country owed their lives to not drinking water. Many stalwart advocates of the *status quo* condemned the growing habit of drinking tea, but it had the very real advantage of ensuring that the tea drinker consumed boiled water. Equally the beer drinker was protected against the ghastly risks he would have run had he taken to 'pure water'.

Home life was practically non-existent. The tenement was a place to sleep, and perhaps to work in. The tavern, beer shop, gin cellar, or something that was daintily named a club, but differed little from these other haunts, was the habitual refuge from such homes in the uneasy and all too brief hours of leisure.

The misfortunes of being a great favourite when the only social meeting place was the tavern or the ale-house was something that James Ward was quite unable to understand. He could not put himself imaginatively in another person's shoes and did not appreciate that most of his father's contemporaries thought heavy drinking a commonplace, every day habit. It was so ordinary as to be quite unremarkable, and the financial disasters that followed were accepted as bad luck.

James' condemnation of his father's mistakes was very severe, though he was incapable of assessing the results of his own errors of judgement on his own vicissitudes. His strictures upon his father were, nevertheless, relieved by a tiny gleam of appreciation. 'My father', he wrote in one of the casual autobiographical notes he made in his old age, 'was an ingenious man – he made a very beautiful Model of one of his Cider Carts – he was the foreman of a large Cider and Fruit Merchants, was a great favourite and everyone expected he would become a Partner, but he took to drinking and lost everything—.'

As so often happens in such families the wife and mother was the leading light and guiding spirit. Like so many London house-wives of the day she let lodgings, though how she was able to do so is not clear. Her lodgers may have been some of the workmen employed in the cellars about the fruit and cider business. Mrs. Ward must perforce do some things for them, and her husband was busy with his drinking. He had no time for business, so she did her best to do his work as well. By so much was her ordinary housework made heavier. It is remarkable that a woman whose early years were spent in such savage and unremitting toil should have lived to a great age.

James' own survival is something of a miracle. Fathers then did not bother their heads about their offspring, and Mrs. Ward must have had little leisure to devote to her children. With the other local children James ran wild about the streets and wharves. Casualties amongst them there must have been, but James was fortunate to escape the injury or death that must have been con-tinuously hovering about his infantile escapades. The Thames was not then embanked in this neighbourhood. The wharves were unfenced and the children gambolled about them in imminent peril of being drowned, or crushed beneath the feet of the gigan-tic horses crashing along the cobblestones hauling great waggons with vast wheels of six or nine inches wide.

James made friends with the bargemen and carters, but it sounds rather apochryphal to suggest that as a child under seven 'he learned riding at the peril of his neck and limbs, knew what it was to shoot a Thames bridge (presumably London Bridge) in a crazy boat with the lee gunwale under water', a spectacle that George Borrow later watched with awe and terror: or 'found out how to use his fists by guarding the contents of his father's vegetable cart from the sneak thieves of Covent Garden'.

Once indeed James narrowly escaped drowning when he fell into the Thames, but he was fished out in time. He suffered a frightful illness as a result, from which only his grand consti-tution enabled him to recover. Once during this illness his mother gave him up for dead. He recovered consciousness to find her holding a mirror to his mouth to confirm her suspicion that he was dead, or prove him alive.

Most dreadful and shocking accidents take place in the monstrous aggregation of mechanical transport that fills the streets of modern London, but eighteenth-century London was just as bad. Horses could easily fall upon the cobbles or become unmanageable. Cattle, sheep and pigs were driven through the streets to market and slaughter-houses. They too could break away from their drovers, and cause death and destruction, or at least add disturbance to the noisy and congested streets. Rabies was not controlled, and the terrifying dash of a slavering mad dog was no unusual sight. Mechanical devices were clumsy and dangerous, and horrible accidents happened like that when Ward saw a hogshead fall on a neighbour who was 'crushed to a mash'. It made a vivid impression upon him, not surprisingly. Being naturally devout he was led to think of the rewards offered in heaven to those who endure cheerfully below. In this he was encouraged by his pious Uncle Thomas. It was the better alternative. He could have become the eighteenth-century pattern of the cosh boy.

James was put to work at an age when a modern child is just commencing school. He says he was only five years old when he began filling bottles from the cider casks in the cellar beneath his father's shop. If this is so, he had collected a remarkable variety of experiences before then. All that is certain is that he was barely out of his babyhood when he began to earn his living.

Though this employment kept him off the streets and protected him from their manifold dangers, it did not remove him from evil moral influences. The adults who corked and sealed the bottles he filled were a crude lot, part and parcel of their class. Their conversation was laced with ribald allusions and lurid phrases, and their habits unclean. Their peculiar sense of humour was tickled when they taught the infant bottle-filler to sing in his childish treble, obscene and ribald songs, the meaning of which he was quite incapable of understanding. Here was a rare example of the incongruity that Bergson declares to be the root of laughter, but the old man who looked back upon his early childhood felt only disgust. He was entirely without the gift of laughter and looked at life with the jaundiced view of a narrow-minded bigot. Many of these songs were amorous, or drinking songs, and some of them were the popular ditties written by Dibden, in which the men, who included his father, were unlikely to have been able to see any harm, any more than we could. It was only the immense prudery of the octogenarian James that could regard this as one more experience of the evil temptations that everywhere beset the good man as he passes through life.

The chronology of these early years is not very clear and now never will be, but throughout this time James' father continued drinking, a habit which does not shrink, but thrives in its own unnatural soil. Every excuse that the habits of the time allow must be made for him. He followed the common road of his contemporaries, though other members of his family behaved very differently, and occupied positions of varying standing in the community. A great uncle is said to have been one of the head clerks of the Bank of England. Another brother-in-law is believed to have invented colour printing. Thomas, an elder brother, was a pious chapel member, who was ceaseless in exhorting James Ward, the father and husband, to mend his ways, drinking that produced hallucinations of the most gruesome pattern based on the old wives' tales that were constantly repeated and believed most fervently.

The age indeed was one of the grossest superstition. The night was filled with the activities of witches, warlocks and ghosts. Few but the wicked stirred abroad after dark. Those who stayed at home were apt to spend the evening recounting stories of the supernatural, of terror by night, of apparitions, wraiths and wonders. James Ward was sent at night to fetch water from a neighbouring well to quench his father's alcoholic drought. This well, the nearest potable water, stood by an empty vault at the end of a dark and noisome lane on one side of which was a charnel house filled with the ghastly intimations of mortality, 'The mouldering bones of dead and gone generations'. James, his infant mind filled with tales of mystery and terror, found these nocturnal errands to the well frightful experiences. Never afterwards could he approach this spot, even in the brightest light of day, without a quaver of apprehension.

These fireside tales and nightly tremors went far to create the mind susceptible to wonders and monstrosities that tainted James' later outlook. It was by no means an unusual defect in an age ready to accept the most palpable frauds of quacks and mystery mongers, some of whose claims were investigated by the august Royal Society. James was confirmed in it by what purported to be a real experience of supernatural visitation, but was really a delusion of alcoholic frenzy.

When he was dying, pious Uncle Thomas tried once more to call his brother James to repentance and a salutary change of habit, but it was not to be. Though he sent for James repeatedly during the last night of his life, that unregenerate brother, perhaps fearing the force of exhortations from a dying man, perhaps for the more likely and less recondite reason that he was dead drunk and incapable, only reached his brother's house after Thomas had passed away. All his superstitious dread and awe were at once aroused and exaggerated by the nervous excitement of the habitual drunkard; the elder James constantly heard his brother's voice thereafter. In terror he abandoned drinking with the result that might have been expected. This violent change in his habits came too late. After such mental disturbance he became a physical wreck, one more victim of time and environment, too weak to withstand the harsh conditions of his day. The reform due to the fantasies of a disordered mind lasted no long time and soon he followed his elder brother to the grave. Seventy years later James still believed in the reality of the ghost of his Uncle Thomas seen by his father, and so did his uncle's relict and children. It was so real to them at the time that they removed to another house. They had been intimidated by hearing Uncle Thomas going about the house with his usual cough, the sound of his step, the tapping of his stick. In one of his many notes on his early life, James tells a tale of what would now be called a poltergeist, though the glass and china it broke at night were whole again in the morning.

When old Ward died the maintenance of the family fell upon Mrs. Ward, who opened a vegetable shop. She already had her children and her lodgers to attend to, so had a very busy life.

James, who had graduated from bottle-filling in the cider cellar to bottle-washing at Three Cranes Wharf, now long since demolished, worked twelve or fourteen hours a day for four shillings a week when he was about nine years old. No doubt many other children of his class and age were then employed under the same conditions perhaps at a variety of jobs. This employment enabled him to help his devoted mother a little. James' fate was not softened by his change of employment. He was not unconscious of the hardships he suffered at this time of his life, and has left a poignant description of the deplorable situation of a little boy that he remembered all his life. He endured his exhausting labour in an everlasting bath of steam and Thames fog, and was tormented by chilblains on his hands and feet, a disability probably due to malnutrition that he had suffered from since his baby days. His master, just though he may have been according to his lights, was brusque and rough as the character of his employees made abundantly necessary. James was not exempted from this treatment, (why should he be?) but as an old man related that the spirits of a child could rise in song even above these circumstances, a truly herculean and astonishing performance.

The shadows of this darkling existence were lightened by the discovery of the pleasures of reading, and by occasional visits to the rural fringes of the town with his employer's vegetable and cider carts. His only attendance at a regular school seems to have been a few weeks at Merchant Taylors just before his father's final débâcle. Yet in his old age he remembered reading *Don Quixote* and *Pilgrim's Progress* when he was first employed as a bottle filler. This is quite incredible. James Ward was by no means a prodigy of learning like John Evelyn's son – who died of it. And few children of five, six, or seven years old can ever have been able to read such books. However he must have read them at some time in his early youth before he was apprenticed to John Raphael Smith, unless his memory was ungovernably faulty. He must have mixed up this detail of his early life as he did many others – a common failing in old men's tales.

He found these two and some cast-aside books of religion

amongst the lumber of his uncle and aunt, and hoarded them
carefully for his own continuing pleasure. Doubtless the Bible
was another standby. James took surreptitious peeps at these
works whenever he could steal a few minutes from his everlasting labour, and so broke down the tedious length of a day that
most moderns would consider impossibly long and unendurable.
James was of sufficiently stout material, but his reading must
have deepened the austerity of his mind besides supporting and
inflating the egoism that is often the character of deeply religious
people.

'Hard work and short commons, fog and chilblains vanished
alike from memory over those enchanted pages, long passages of
which live in my memory even to the end of my lengthening
days,' is his own description of this heavenly relief from earthly
hardship.

The trips to the neighbouring countryside introduced him to
sights and sounds very different from the chaotic and tumbling
life of Thames Street, and his young mind was at once formidably
impressed with the rural scenes that later on were to provide him
with so many themes for painting.

'When I was about five years old I was suffered to go in a cart
through Deptford and Greenwich', he wrote in a document now
no longer among his papers, but quoted by Julia Frankau, 'and I
can now picture myself seated in the middle of a load of apples,
turnips and carrots, hearing a man bawling through the villages
and myself enjoying the sights of the shipping, with all the rude
clamour of the streets. At the same age I was sent with a man to
deliver cider at a place called Pratt's Bottom in Kent. The effect
on my infant mind is beyond description. It was a small public
house on the roadside of an old fashioned style, between two
hills; at the front of a large green covered with young Willows,
with plenty of Sheep, Geese, Fowls, etc., and before to the right
a Farrier's and Wheelwright's shop with the clinking of hammers
and wheelwrights at work, and from which there was a rude gate
or style leading up to a large overhanging wood ascending to the
top of the hill. The weather was beautiful, and here I was put to
bed. As soon as it was light I was waked by the lowing of a cow

after her calf. The noise was so new and odd that I tumbled out of bed and clambered up the old fashioned window step to see what it was, and when I looked out it appeared as if I had got into heaven itself. I know not how I huddled on my petticoats, but I was on the green almost before I knew it and my first gambol was to run among the geese who soon began to hiss around me to my great delight. But the Inn-keeper seeing the danger I was in, soon came, and taking me quietly by the hand, led me into the house, surprised that he should thus take me from all my delights.'

The importance of this occasion can be exaggerated. Every youngster is interested in the sights and sounds of the farmyard and runs to play with the animals and birds, especially if they are young like himself. The most sophisticated find the charm of young life difficult to resist. The awkward gambols of a colt, or the quaint jerky jumps of a lamb are equally ludicrous and attractive, so some of James' later enthusiasm must be discounted, unless this youthful and instantaneous appreciation of the rural scene is taken as no more than a healthy normal reaction.

James described only two of these journeys, but he must have made more, if infrequently. These trips were a holiday from and a welcome interlude to the arduous labours of bottle-filling or washing. They were an invaluable dose of natural and wholesome enjoyment, an antidote to the bleak surroundings of his everyday life. Memories of these happy days gave him something else to think about besides the immanence of death.

Political events are not likely to interest a child, least of all one like James Ward. The country was in a depressed and chaotic state. Few people were able to understand why this was so. The causes of the American War of Independence and the subsequent war with France in all the known corners of the earth were beyond the ken of anyone but a handful of the limited ruling and professional class. Defeat in America and the disturbance of trade caused by a world-wide war, brought England to the brink of disaster. The mob felt the consequences in growing hardship, but knew no more of it than that they suffered because something, they knew not what, was wrong with the state of the country.

One thing did arouse the fury of the people, contemptuously referred to as the mob. There was a movement for tolerance towards the small minority of Catholics, resulting in an Act of 1778 for the removal of some of their disabilities in England. The introduction of a bill for a similar measure in Scotland aroused the violent Protestant feeling in that country. Riots broke out in Edinburgh, and the half insane Lord George Gordon, brother to the Duke of Gordon, became the head of a Protestant Association that besieged the House with petitions for the repeal of the Act and throwing out the Bill. A great meeting was held in St. George's Fields, and a huge petition was carried through the streets of London in procession to be laid before Parliament.

Little James Ward may not have left his bottle-washing to follow this procession, but as the days passed the people became inflamed by Gordon's wild oratory until they were at a pitch of frenzy. This was the more easy at a time when gin was the common tipple of the poor, and when most of the community looked at life through an alcoholic haze. And indeed the 'mob', that is the working class regarded rioting as their right. It was the only means of protest against their grievances.

Even in the lobbies of the House there were scenes of violence. The eighteenth century mob was dangerous. There was for practical purposes no police, and in times of riot the military had to be called out. On the 2nd June 1780 several houses belonging to Catholics were destroyed and a Catholic chapel in Moorfields was sacked and burned on the following Sunday, the magistrates and military being unable or unwilling to protect it. Next day a few rioters were arrested and cast into Newgate prison. The mob went mad, and few of London's workers can have failed to join it if only to watch events. Little James Ward was almost certainly amongst them. He was then eleven years old, and according to his own story, had been a worker since the age of five.

The town was given up to riot and destruction for the next four days. More Catholic houses and chapels were destroyed on the Monday, on Tuesday scarcely a shop was opened. Blue ribbons were worn by the respectable as a sign of their adherence to the true religion, and 'No Popery' was chalked up on doors to prevent the destruction of houses. Grimaldi, an Italian actor, recently arrived in London, declared on his door 'No religion', and a Houndsditch Jew 'This house is a sound Protestant'.

The resentment of the mob centred round Newgate Prison, and on Tuesday evening it was attacked and set on fire. Some three hundred prisoners, many of the most degenerate characters, were let loose. During this rioting a distillery on Holborn Hill, belonging to a Mr. Langdale, a Catholic, was destroyed, and the raw spirit flooded the streets where it flowed down the gutters like water. The excitement of the rioters was by so much increased. They had been drinking more than usual, but even in that day it was an extraordinary sight to see men and women guzzling raw spirits from the gutters, and falling unconscious in the muck of the streets. The more sober continued to sack the houses of known Catholics, and to make bonfires of their household furniture, as well as to attack prisons and release the prisoners. The soldiers and militia looked on with arms in their hands, and did nothing to terminate the disorder. The magistrates were either too frightened or too supine to give the necessary orders though their inaction may have been founded in sympathy with the aims of the rioters.

All that night the sky over London was red with the reflection of flames of burning houses and possessions, and only at the Bank was there sufficient action to prevent the mob storming it. The dawn of the next day broke as upon a city suddenly taken possession of by a hostile and barbarous army. At last orders were given and the troops set to work. During Thursday the rioters were dispersed, with over two hundred dead and wounded. At the subsequent trials twenty unlucky ones were condemned to death, though they could have been no more guilty than hundreds of other people. Their misfortune was to be selected as an example.

The leader of the rioters, or their inspiration, was thrown into the Tower and tried for High Treason, but escaped on a plea of insanity. Some years later he abandoned Christianity, and embraced Judaism, an action a Victorian writer believed to confirm his insanity conclusively.

Through these scenes of riot and disorder the child may have

B

wandered dangerously, more dangerously than when he had played in the street and on the wharf at an even earlier age. Such scenes as that depicted in Wheatley's striking picture of the riots at their height must have made an indelible impression on Ward's mind. Nowhere in his anecdotes of his youth does he mention this event, but he could not possibly have escaped its impact, although it was not personal enough for him to deem it worthy of remark.

In Ward's childhood too, numbers of criminals, a few guilty of the most abominable crimes, but many of only trivial mis-demeanours, were condemned to death, and publicly executed. The scaffold outside Newgate and the passage of the Tyburn cart were almost daily spectacles. People gathered in thousands to watch these inspiring sights, and groaned with anguish at the death of a hardened sinner who put on a good show, or booed deliriously at the trembling take-off of a craven. James Ward would have been a singular boy if he never partook of these enjoyments.

Soon after the Gordon riots a change took place in James' circumstances that determined the whole of his future life. It happened in the casual way such things do. The opportunity occurred and it was taken. There was no more to it than that.

On the one hand it has been said that James occupied his meal times and leisure from bottle-washing, in carpentering and basket-making as well as his own professedly assiduous reading in the Bible, *Pilgrim's Progress*, *Don Quixote*, and so on. The leisure available to a child who worked from 6 a.m. to 6 or 8 p.m. must have been rather scanty for all these hobbies. Grundy declared that he was in the habit of sketching the objects that passed his window – recollect that they were seen through a window blurred inside with steam and outside by Thames fog. Was this done in time snatched from bottle-filling? 'These transcriptions from life', Grundy continues, 'are described by an early biog-rapher as being full at once of the vigour, the vivacity and the diffidence of talent.' I have not been able to trace this early biographer, but this statement fills me with doubt. To my mind an untrained child could hardly have produced such sketches. I prefer Julia Frankau's idea that James' apprenticeship to John Raphael Smith was an accident quite uninfluenced by any inherent artistic talent Ward possessed. There was an opportunity – that was all.

William Ward, James' elder brother, was just at the end of his term of apprenticeship, under Smith, who consequently had a vacancy for a pupil. What could be more natural than that the place should be given to James? He undertook to serve two years longer than usual as a recompense for paying no premium. Both brothers recognised that this was a craft that held more prospects than bottle-washing in a cider cellar, and it removed James from the purlieus of Thames Street to the comparative comfort of Oxford Street. The artist's struggle in life had begun.

CHAPTER II

The Apprenticeship Years

James Ward's apprenticeship to John Raphael Smith rescued him
from Thames Street. He found himself in the much more congenial neighbourhood of Oxford Road, now Oxford Street. He was
not noticeably grateful for the change, nor was he satisfied for
very long. He speedily found causes for discontent in his new
place. He failed to realise the sacrifices his brother, William, had
made to secure him a chance to work with him under Smith.

In the later years of the eighteenth century the production of
mezzotints was more often a co-operative job done by a master
and his employees and apprentices, junior and senior, than the
work of a single person. The more employees a master engraver
had the greater his output, and consequently the greater his
income. Under the guidance of his master, William Ward had
become a competent engraver, and his services to Smith must
have been of great value.

John Raphael Smith was a type of the successful master engraver of the day, and his arrangement with the Wards displays
his business acumen. He had begun life as a draper, and had
learned the art of dealing in that undertaking. He was a successful dealer in his own wares as well as in the production of those
who worked for, or were apprenticed to him. When James
joined him he had recently taken a shop and house, No. 83
Oxford Road, and here he entertained his customers by exhibiting
in his drawing room, the pictures he was engraving. Smith was
one of those oddities that were so prevalent before the machine
age, as indeed was Ward himself. He was an excellent man of
business. He was great at his job, and has been called a man of
genius. His output was enormous. He had, too, a flair for social

life, and found time to cut a notable figure in the *beau monde*, the real world of art and fashion. Alas the standard of uniformity created by a technological society has abolished this feature of English society. After 200 years it has been possible for Montague Allwood to pronounce that once 'it was a feature of English society that it could produce individuals who do not challenge the social order'. Such a one was John Raphael Smith and another was James Ward. There were many others in a society where individuality was admired especially if the individual was rich or notorious: but today is an age of conformity but conformity to what is difficult to say.

Living and working in the house of such a man as Smith must have been a cataclysmic change from a bottle-washing cellar at Three Cranes Wharf. His escape from bottle-washing to the humble tasks of an apprentice living in the master's home did not appear to him as any form of liberation. Already he was convinced of his great worth to the world, his native egotism having been greatly accentuated by his reading. It was of the kind that must turn his thoughts inward, to dwell upon the necessity of saving his own soul from the dreadful torments of hell.

To any ordinary mind sweeping out a shop devoted to the sale of pictures, running errands for the master, waiting at table, doing some scullion's work, the sleeping under the counter in the best manner of the traditional London apprentice, would have been a heavenly change from sordid and savage toil in the wine cellar. Not so James Ward! He, who had slaved so for a pittance since his early childhood, must needs resent his new conditions.

Out of doors he might have lived in a different country. Thames Street and its neighbourhood was a slum, the atmosphere poisoned, the dingy buildings often in a dangerous state of repair. Oxford Street must have been cleaner and more savoury. There were fields a few steps away. Building did not extend very far north in the 1780's. What had been done was laid out in the fine system of squares that are a lesson to modern town planners. To the west George Street and Hanover Square had been built in 1718–1719. Cavendish Square about the same time, and Manchester

Square about 1770. Portman Square and Bedford Square were
built in the 1760's, as was Charlotte Street, where John Wilkes'
chariot could often be seen waiting outside the house of his
mistress at about the same date as James Ward came to Oxford
Street. Portland Place was built in 1778, and Russell Square in
1805. To the north west was Mr. William's farm at Mary-le-
bonne park, the largest in the county of Middlesex, upwards of
five-hundred acres. Beyond Portland Place was the open space,
afterwards landscaped and made into Regent's Park. Further on
was Primrose Hill where the Welsh immigrants to London, or
perhaps some devoted antiquarians amongst them, held the first
Druidic Eisteddfodd in the 1770's. Chalk Farm was really a farm
then, and Swiss Cottage a cottage.

Living in Oxford Street in the 1780's was not far short of
living in the country, especially when compared with the purlieus
of Thames Street. So far, however, James Ward, whose eye was
determinedly turned inward, would not acknowledge this, nor
indeed did he display any interest. His mind, if his later recollections of these days can be trusted, was concentrated upon the
lack of recognition of his as yet undisplayed genius, and the
miserable and degrading duties of an apprentice.

The place was chock-a-block with all the apparatus of the
artist's and engraver's trades. Famous pictures were brought in
for engraving, pictures by artists who ranged downwards from
the great president of the Royal Academy, Sir Joshua Reynolds
himself. Besides these pictures there were all the miscellaneous
oddments that collect in studios, fine materials of brilliant design,
grotesque lay figures, paintings and engravings in all states, a
world to stimulate, perhaps over-stimulate, a vivid imagination
like that of James Ward.

As an apprentice James saw many famous people, both customers and artists, who visited Smith's shop. They were doubtless
indifferent enough to the apprentice who assisted Smith to wait
on them, but he was far from indifferent to them. He envied
their airs and graces, *bon ton*, the self-confident bearing of the
well-to-do and respectable, many of whom were recognised
members of the fashionable world.

Many years later Ward related that none of them was interested in him or aware of his potentialities as an artist, and was still resentful of this indifference. At the time he consoled himself in his own peculiar way with his fixed idea that he would one day be as great and famous as they, which was really not far wrong.

Amongst these people was Henry Fuseli, the half-mad Swiss painter of fantastic and morbid studies, who has awaited the present day to be regarded as a forerunner of such men as Rodin, Gauguin and Van Gogh. John Raphael Smith made a good thing out of Fuseli. The latter revenged himself by a criticism of Smith's engravings of his Shakespeare illustrations, outspoken to the point of insult. Never very restrained in his behaviour Fuseli rampaged into Smith's studio one day when Ward was present, and declaimed against Smith's presumption in 'toning down' some of the eccentricities of his pictures. He was particularly incensed by a bad proof of his *Lady Macbeth*.

Ward's admiration of Fuseli's angry declamations, punctuated by his affected stammer, made the more impressive by his 'foreign air', was changed to wonder when the artist seized a piece of chalk and dashed off a sketch of a gigantic female hand and arm during the height of his wild harangue. This performance seemed a marvel to young James. Like most children would, if so strongly impressed as he was, James at once set out to imitate the performance.

As soon as Fuseli had taken his eccentric self away Ward declared that he seized a piece of chalk and drew the hand and arm on the front of a print. Naturally his brother William saw this drawing and wanted to know who had made it. At first he thought James was joking when he claimed to be the artist. He did not believe it possible that James could have drawn it, and particularly not from memory. James was finally able to convince his brother.

There is nothing whatever to confirm this astonishing statement, but on the contrary every reason to suppose William had accepted willingly the conditions under which he learned his trade. He had acquired the craft well enough under Smith's tuition. He was a much more ordinary person than James. For one thing he had learned discipline at Merchant Taylors School, a very different introduction to life from James' bottle-washing and filling. William was a man of talent; James a man of genius, dowered in his own opinion with quite exceptional gifts. His opinion was confirmed by his later performances, though not accepted by the world quite as decidedly as by his own majestic egotism. William's work was painstaking, never rising to inspiration nor falling below excellence. He was in fact a competent engraver and therefore of great value to Raphael Smith. He engraved Morland's *The Anglers Repast* in 1780, before he had completed his apprenticeship. He was highly esteemed by Sir Walter Gilbey who calls him 'the famous engraver', and suggests that he may have known George Morland before the Ward family removed to Kensal Green.

In his numerous unrelated notes about his time with John Raphael Smith Ward complains bitterly of the treatment he received. His precocious, unacknowledged genius was terribly irked by the life of an apprentice. He became very conscious of his gifts as an artist. Later he complained that Smith would not give him any instruction in drawing nor allow him to use any paper for drawing exercises except the rotten backs of unfinished proofs. These would not take the chalk.

Grundy, quoting a letter written to Sir Charles Eastlake in Ward's eighty-ninth year, said that Ward described himself as 'a tiny little boy, timid, diffident'. So he probably was. He had been overworked, possibly underfed, since infancy. His childhood could hardly have been happy. His hell-fire religion was no compensation for physical discomfort and the stories about ghosts and devils that haunted his childish imagination. Later this pre-occupation proved a great handicap to the full development of his powers. Physically Ward never attained average height, though in manhood he was cast in a sturdy mould. His timidity must have rapidly disappeared as he became familiar with the new and stimulating environment. Smith failed to notice this trait in his character. He had no hesitation in sending this small boy on a journey to Norwich, then no small undertaking for a grown

man, to collect a valuable hunter and bring it home. The horse
had of course to travel to its new owner by road and under its
own power. Where had James learned sufficient horse sense to
enable him to carry out such an errand successfully? The
question is unanswerable, but the fact does not support James'
claim to timidity. It is rather evidence of great staunchness.

James' complaints about Smith's conduct towards him, which
was probably very little different from his treatment of any other
apprentice, culminated in an unbelievable statement made in a
letter written long after in 1847. 'William could not bear'
James wrote, 'to see him suffer under the same tyranny as
himself.' The fact is probably that James ragged his less temperamental brother until William found the situation in Smith's
workshop unbearable. This must have been at about the time
William finished his apprenticeship. On the other hand William
realised that James possessed a large share of talent. He perceived an opportunity to set up in business for himself, and to
employ James profitably.

To do this he needed, as all these craftsmen engravers did, an
apprentice. James, though likely to prove difficult, was the
obvious choice, and William came to an agreement with Smith
to release his brother; but Smith, too, was an astute business man,
and he only agreed to allow James to transfer his indentures on
condition that William agreed to work for him three days a week
at a not unreasonable wage.

The remainder of the week William was at liberty to work for
himself.

Both brothers left Smith's house and went to live in lodgings in
Wells Street off Oxford Street, conveniently near to Smith's
shop. Here they lived till about 1785. During this time William
devoted his agreed three days a week to Smith's work, and it has
been suggested that many of the engravings published by Smith
then were either wholly or partly William's work. This would be
natural enough in the contemporary organisation of the craft, and
is nothing to cavil at, though it makes the precise identification
of each man's contribution to the art of the mezzotint engraver
difficult.

The change according to James, was not satisfactory. It introduced him to a new kind of suffering, the misery of loneliness, an acute trial to a boy of fifteen years or so, especially one so morbid and introspective as he was. Julia Frankau says James went with his brother to Smith's studio on the three days a week William worked there. If he did he must have collected many useful hints. There is no doubt that his introduction to engraving had fired his ambition to become a famous man. He followed that ambition with unremitting industry and zeal, the solid foundation on which his later reputation rested.

James' own tale of this period is quite different. According to him he was left quite alone in William's garret workroom, and kept constantly laying mezzotint grounds, dreadful drudgery to a mind then all imagination. His only relief was breeding rabbits and birds, and making a flower garden in the workroom window. The window box is easily understood. It was commonplace enough, but breeding birds and animals in a garret not so conventional.

As so often happens the lodging house where the Wards lived was kept by a reduced genteel family of sisters. They added to their income by dressmaking. One of them afterwards married William Say, the engraver. These young women took pity on the lonely boy. He became a great favourite with them, and was invited to spend his evenings with them playing forfeits, riddles and puzzles. He must have expatiated largely upon art, and his exaggerated prudery, that never failed him upon other occasions, so far deserted him one evening, that he fetched down an antique cast of a man in order to demonstrate some point in his theory of beauty, 'quite unconscious of the sly giggle that passed between a large circle of young ladies on such an open display'. Not all his evenings were spent so pleasantly in parlour games and aesthetic dialectic to an admiring circle of feminine youth, a delightful audience for a young man. Some were spent at an evening school in the neighbouring Castle Street, learning to write.

This recollection gives Ward another chance to bemoan his early fate. 'I have ever regretted', he wrote, 'that there was no kind friend to come forward in the midst of my earlier drudgery to have got me into some charity school. For want of this a very extraordinary timidity haunted me to such a degree, as to prevent my ever writing before others, lest the spelling should be wrong, and that, from a peculiarity of sentiment, appeared as a crime.' If the volume of his correspondence is any criterion he fully conquered his early diffidence. Indeed the chaotic spelling of such famous people as Nollelkins and Benjamin West, not to speak of society as a whole, might have reassured James, who was quite unnecessarily concerned.

Whether he went to Smith's studio with his brother during these years or not, James must have seen some of the other outstanding personalities whose business brought them to the shop while he was an apprentice. Amongst these were some fine eighteenth-century oddities.

Ward's experience with Fuseli was striking. The Rev. Matthew William Peters was no less a character. He was a successful cleric and managed to combine that profession with the painting of 'nude and beautiful women'. Peters was the son of Matthew Peters, a civil engineer, who wrote three books on farming, and is said to have laid out the grounds and gardens at Stowe. Some of Peters' pictures were engraved by Smith, and Peters must have visited the studio while Ward was a boy there. Painting occupied him more seriously than holy orders during the early part of his life. He became distinguished enough to be the subject of satire by Dr. Wolcot, writing as 'Peter Pindar', and of a touch by Anthony Pasquin.

Peters was a pattern of the worldly eighteenth-century cleric who managed to combine success in the church with a marked Calvinism and a career as a painter. Among the subjects he painted for Boydell's Shakespeare was one of the *Merry Wives* that shows him possessed of a sprightly humour. Though mainly attracted by the intricacies of recondite costume, a *Florentine Lady in Pisan Dress, Mr. Wortly Montague in the dress of an Arabian Prince* and so on, Peters' *Country Girl* may have attracted Ward's notice. Peters' life was more or less orthodox. He studied art in Dublin, progressed from there to a premium of the Society for the Encouragement of Arts, and so to his modest fame.

Another wit whose work was engraved by Smith was Richard Cosway, son of the master of the public school at Tiverton. He must paint, so his father and earliest patron, Oliver Peard, paid for him to learn under Thomas Hudson, Sir Joshua Reynolds' master. Leaving here, Cosway, still a boy, went to Shipley's drawing academy in the Strand, where he was employed as a waiter to carry tea and other refreshments for the students. He must have been an engaging child because some of them, Nollekins and others, gave him drawing lessons, and encouraged him to enter for a Society of Arts premium. He won five guineas. Later he won others. This led to his employment as a teacher in Parr's school where he occupied his leisure in doing heads for shops and fancy miniatures, not always quite chaste, to be used in the lids of snuff boxes carried by the fops and young men of fashion. He earned a great deal of money, and frequented the gayest company in town. In a word 'from one of the dirtiest of boys he became one of the smartest of men'. He was often to be seen at Christie's dressed in sword and bag, wearing a small three-cornered hat on the top of his powdered toupé and a mulberry silk coat profusely embroidered with strawberries, quite justifying the portrait by Dighton of *The Maccaroni Painter, or Billy Dimple sitting for his picture*. Cosway dealt in old pictures as well as painting. His own self-portrait depicted what he would have liked to be rather than what he was. In the height of his success he lived at 20 Stratford Place where fashionable people made his studio a morning lounge, gratified by the acquaintance of the painter, and the splendour of the furniture he provided for their comfort. The Prince of Wales' carriage was frequently to be seen at his door. James Ward must have been dazzled when such a mould of fashion lounged into Smith's studio, dangling his clouded cane on a silken ribbon and taking snuff from a box decorated with one of his own 'galant', indecorous, amusing miniatures.

Contrast as the Macaroni must have been in appearance to the parson in his bands it can have been no greater contrast than that he made with 'Geoffrey Gambado', the horseman, writer, amateur artist and caricaturist, Henry Bunbury. Smith en-

graved his work and he must have called at the shop. Henry was
the son of the Rev. Sir William Bunbury, Bart., of Mildenhall,
Suffolk, and his taste for the absurd was evident from his childhood. He began to make humorous drawings while still at
Westminster School, one of a boy riding on a pig. At Cambridge
he guyed dons and undergraduates alike, picking upon ungainly
and awkward habits, in pencil or chalk drawings. He made a
series of burlesque illustrations for that most humourous book
Tristram Shandy, and for others. Some hints for bad horsemen
was a series engraved by Smith. Then came an *Academy for
Grown Horsemen* by Geoffrey Gambado with twelve plates and
a portrait of the author, a folio, 1787, followed by *Annals of
Horsemanship* in 1791. Both were volumes of equestrian misadventures of which a third edition with illustrations engraved
by Rowlandson came out in 1808. Rowlandson etched *Anglers of
1811* as well, and Gilray was engaged upon *A Barber's Shop* just
before he lapsed into hopeless idiocy.

When he came into the studio Bunbury was a genial soul
possessed of great charm. This may have led him to notice
Smith's apprentice with a salute of casual, general friendliness
that the son of a baronet and a recognised painter could afford to
bestow upon all and sundry. These qualities endeared him to
everybody. Benjamin West, President of the Royal Academy,
flattered him, and that prince of snobs, Horace Walpole, compared him to Hogarth, a comparison that had slight justification.
If he ever did speak to Ward in Smith's studios, James must have
glowed with satisfaction for Bunbury was all that he was not.
He was a friend of the distinguished, of Goldsmith, Garrick, and
Reynolds, and he was a man of family and education, who went
into any society as an equal. This was quite enough for Ward to
admire or envy, although Bunbury's humour was only the
rough and ready drollery then in vogue, depending upon absurd
contrasts, ludicrous distortions, horseplay and personal mis-
adventure.

These and many others must have visited the studio while
James was a boy there. He was by his nature alternately stirred
to admiration by their posings and achievements, and driven to

burning envy by his own conception of his yet unfulfilled capacity for work of equal, if not greater, merit.

Although James was so critical in his old age of Smith and looked back upon him as a tyrant, his only foundation for the accusation was very slight. He was once thrashed by Smith when he lost a pet terrier that he had usually taken with him when running Smith's errands. Doubtless James resented this as any punished child might, but it does not go far to justify him in declaring Smith to have been haughty and tyrannical.

Neither William Ward nor Smith had anything against each other. On the contrary they were friends, and when Smith went to live at Kensal Green, William Ward followed suit. William had become prosperous enough to provide for his family, and to remove his mother and sisters from the depressing environment and drudgery of the vegetable shop in the city.

Kensal Green was then an isolated, straggling hamlet some distance from the verge of London, separated from the metropolis by fields and lanes. It was partly in the parish of Hammersmith, partly in Paddington. James joined his brother and the rest of the family there. The new neighbourhood was a healthy change for Ward's mother and two of his three sisters.

The third sister was already married. She entered into matrimony very early, and James was glad. As a child she had teased him unmercifully; in his own words, 'my childish years was rendered very tormenting, being very timid'. She went off with her husband, and James lost sight of her altogether. 'My impression is,' he added, 'that he was an engraver, named Williams, a friend of my brother's. I never knew what became of him or where he died, but some years back [from 1847] Henry Morland called upon me to know if I could tell that particular – as Mrs. Williams was alive and had married another man – and there was some property she could get if she could tell the particulars of his death – which it appeared she knew as little of as I know myself.' This is very curious, and suggests that Ward's sister parted from her first husband before his death, though the point is of no great importance unless to demonstrate some casualness in marital relations at that time. The family had no great regard for their sister.

Another puzzle emerges from this move. It has been suggested that James Ward senior died in delirium tremens shortly after the death of his pious brother Thomas, whose ghost, a fantasy of alcoholic frenzy, haunted James and pursued him to a miserable and tormented death-bed within twelve months. When the family moved to Kensal Green the elder James is said to have lived with them, to have been subjected to practical jokes by his son James and George Morland. His favourite occupation was to sit in the 'Chimney corner with a tankard of liquor by his side, smoking a long pipe'.

The change from the solitary introspection of the Wells Street garret to a somewhat crowded family life must have been most salutary for James. Surrounded by half a dozen of his closest relatives and constantly in their company, his mental balance ought to have been restored, but nothing could repair the damage that had been done to his psyche by the hardships of his childhood, not even the pleasant, almost trivial, tasks that now occupied so much of his day.

His love of animals had found some fulfilment in Wells Street among his rabbits and birds, and the mechanical ability he had inherited from his father found expression in making rabbit hutches, bird cages and flower cabinets. These he designed him-self and continuously improved and adorned with carving, with sufficient success to give him great satisfaction. It was the sort of satisfaction commonly sought by a solitary introspective lad, and does not lead to a proper comparison of his powers with those of other young men. This lack of competition gave him a false idea of his own achievements and encouraged him to think himself quite exceptional, something in which he needed no encourage-ment. In Wells Street his mechanical ability had found an outlet with the simple construction of rabbit hutches and so on. It found a wider field at Kensal Green. James is said to have built himself a boat in which he sailed upon a pond in the grounds, doubtless imagining himself on far voyages into wild seas, but a pond large enough for this hobby at or near Kensal Green seems improbable. Nearly all very old men have fantasies about their youth.

Life in the country at Kensal Green was an entirely new experience for James. Besides constant companionship all the sights
and scenes of the countryside that were to play so great a part in
his future were immediately before his eyes. The casual enthusiasm aroused by his infant visits to Pratt's Bottom and other
parts of Kent now became a permanent feature of his life. He
took immense pleasure in constituting himself groom to his
brother's horses and poultry, and gardener to the household.
There is a legend that a party of gypsies made off with all the
poultry one dark night. This depredation was probably not final.
It was easy enough to replace poultry then, although the farm
was not very far from town, a miserable hotbed of crime and
destitution. Consequently the livestock required close guarding.

William Ward was still working for John Raphael Smith and
the close neighbourhood of the two families led to many errands
between them for James. He did odd jobs for both households.
There was no longer any constraint because of James' change of
apprenticeship. He worked on plates for Smith, went rook shooting with him, and was thrown a good deal into the society of his
guests. He saw much of the sort of living he had found so disgusting in his father's house. Smith was a wild liver as well as a
hugely industrious engraver. The manners of the day did nothing
to reduce his rake-helly way of life.

James, who abhorred this moral atmosphere, was thrown back
more and more upon the consolation of religion. His serious cast of
mind was laughed at by his relations and their circle, and they
tried to undermine his principles by getting him to read Voltaire
and Tom Paine. His refuge from these iconoclasts was Young's
Night Thoughts and Paley's *Christian Evidences*; literature that
made a great impression upon his adolescent enthusiasm.

A new and very important influence was brought to bear on
James at Kensal Green. George Morland became acquainted with
the family.

Smith had published engravings of Morland's pictures and
doubtless it was when visiting him that Morland became a friend
of the Wards. At Kensal Green he was a constant visitor and
eventually took lodgings with the family. Though Morland had

already been sufficiently erratic and had just missed a matrimonial adventure with a girl in domestic service whose father was a tailor, he was then an industrious and engaging person. He speedily became enamoured of Ward's sister Anne.

Stimulated by his passion for Anne, encouraged by William Ward, and the general atmosphere of congenial company, Morland worked earnestly. At this time he produced several works rather in the moral tone of Hogarth. They were the first of the long series of rustic scenes of commonplace homeliness which he continuously produced until the day of his death.

George became something of a hero to James Ward, who was his companion in all sorts of escapades, and in the practical jokes that were so marked a feature of the domestic humour of the rather alcoholic boisterousness of the day.

George Morland had a sister Maria. She inspired the love of the sedate and practical William Ward, less exuberant but more lasting than his sister had excited in the more effervescent heart of George. Both couples were soon married. A double wedding was celebrated at St. Pauls, Hammersmith, in October 1786, the entries in the parish register following one another. The two couples set up house together in Kensal Green, an idyllic arrangement, but not destined to be permanent. Such arrangements rarely last. One great disadvantage of life in Kensal Green was that both husbands and wives had to make frequent visits to London. If they were delayed the journey home in darkness, through unlit lanes, was likely to be hazardous. The fringes of London were infested by footpads and cutpurses as well as the High Tobyman, the cream of his dubious profession, the mounted highwayman. The last is a romantic figure today, but must have been terrifying to meet on a dark night.

Mutual fears for each others' safety oppressed these young husbands and wives. Whilst the men felt that the long and lonely road between London and Kensal Green was not safe enough for their wives to travel alone, they could not always escort them because they were engaged in profitable work. The young women feared for their husbands who did not always return home until late at night.

There was no cure for this, but to move back to London. For
a while they lived together in the High Street, Marylebone. Such
an arrangement has obvious disadvantages as so many families
have discovered in these latter days. Quarrels broke out between
the women, and almost resulted in a duel between the men.
After that they obviously could not go on living together. The
Wards went off to Warren Place, Kentish Town, and the Morlands
to a lodging in Great Portland Street. The Ward's father and
mother had probably moved out to Hendon by then.

The influence that association with George Morland had upon
James Ward's development was very marked. James had the
greatest admiration for George and took delight in seeing him
paint, though he subscribes to the current story that Morland
was then painting nudes as pot boilers. James deplored this
occupation as a fall from moral grace, and went so far as to say
that a young man of his age should not have been allowed to see
such pictures, another sign of the prurience of a prude. If George
Morland did indeed paint nudes or pictures of a character to
justify Ward's 'this dire evil', none remain to us.

James acknowledged that despite his many oddities of behaviour while with them George was ever hard at work, and was
good natured, pleasant and lively in disposition. One of his
quirks was to attend his own wedding with a pair of pistols in his
belt. This is odd, but for all we know the road from Kensal Green
to Hammersmith Church may have been dangerous enough to
justify going armed.

William was less severe than James. He attributed Morland's
antics to the fire of genius and felt that after his marriage he
would settle down into a fine character. This prophecy proved
correct for a time, but when his wife gave birth to a still-born
child, the tragedy, coupled with his wife's long illness, completely unsettled him. When he learned that Mrs. Morland
could never have another child he began to frequent the
Britannia, the Mother Redcap tea gardens (now a pub) and the
Assembly Rooms at Kentish Town. At these places he could
indulge his taste for music, but could not avoid its then inevitable accompaniment of heavy drinking.

James could not sufficiently condemn his brother-in-law's conduct. He attributed it to foolishness developed from too rapid success. 'His sudden reputation was more than he could bear and he took to drinking, which ruined him, but gave me a disgust to drink.'

This intimate association with Morland gave James a desire to paint his first pictures, deplorable as he considered the moral and religious atmosphere that Morland lived in. George Morland must have had some leaning to James Ward because James was allowed to watch George painting. Morland had the strongest possible objection to allowing other artists to see him at work, though he could hardly have prevented the people he was living with from doing so. The admiration that James so freely gave was flattering. At first George was ready to give his young companion help, but this he afterwards refused to do. James with his usual egotism and unlimited self-conceit put this down to jealousy. He thought George feared to be eclipsed. James may have been partly justified because some of his paintings were afterwards sold as Morland's, so sedulous an ape was he.

The refusal is much more likely to have been founded on the opposition of the two men's characters. Although he had joined George in some of his pranks, James was already set in his ways. His mind was rigid and inflexible, incapable of the light-hearted attitute towards life that was so fundamental in George's outlook. A careless, jovial rake, George readily made friends with all sorts of men. James, of his own choice, developed a much stronger ability to make enemies. His unbending fanaticism could find no contact with such a different man. Like so many ignorant young men he was so convinced of his own rectitude that he was never tired of preaching. Morland must have grown very bored with sermons on sobriety, a virtue he had no intention of practising in spite of twenty Jameses. James' own family found his continual exhortations exceedingly tedious. There is little wonder that George Morland refused to accept James as an apprentice. He absolutely declined to saddle himself with such an incompatible youth for a couple of years. This was in 1791, when James finished his time with William.

During his apprenticeship with his brother, James had learnt his trade as a mezzotinter excellently well. He was drivingly industrious, and was fully appreciated by William, whose output was increasing by leaps and bounds, no doubt assisted by James' growing expertise. In the late 1780's William's confidence in his brother and protégé allowed James to execute whole plates by himself. These were published as William's work, just as some of William's work, done when serving his time in Smith's studios, had been published by Smith as his own. William gave James special freedom in completing plates that included landscape. A quotation from the now vanished biography of 1807, which is believed to have either been written or inspired by James himself, explains that for landscapes he had 'always evinced a peculiar taste and without which perhaps we should never have seen that character of Nature attempted in mezzotint.' A pronouncement of doubtful validity.

Besides this anonymous work for his brother, a commonplace of the trade then, James made some engravings after Morland during the last years of his time. These were *Children at Play*, 1789, *Cottagers*, and *Travellers*, 1791. This story is probably true, because William, who was living when James made the statement, would have contradicted it if untrue. Again James' technique in these works did not more closely resemble William's than any other early plates known to be by James, e.g. *Rustic Felicity*, the *Rocking Horse*, and *Sunset, Leicestershire*.

The events of the world at large usually meant very little to James Ward. One did. It was the French Revolution. His interest was awakened not by the magnitude of the event, but for much more personal reasons. The disappearance of the French aristocracy destroyed his market. The engravings he and his brother had been making had sold well in that country. They were copies of the old masters, engravings after Morland, and one or two paintings James made in imitation of Morland that William engraved. No wonder this epochal event even impressed James. It hit him in the pocket.

Everything that James did must be romantic in his own mind or else the result of some quite unanticipated chance. It was not good enough for him to think that his environment made him a painter. Something much more cataclysmic was necessary to bolster his ego. First, Fuseli's monstrous sketch of a female arm told him he could draw, or so he discovered when he copied it; second, years later, one of Copley's pictures that was being engraved by the Wards was damaged; James took it upon himself to repair it. To his delighted astonishment he found himself a natural painter. His work could not be distinguished from the original. Amazing! And this was not wholly untrue!

When James began painting his first efforts showed great promise. Though he was unmistakably making an imitation of Morland, there was no doubt his work could well be a mirror for that artist's work. Morland, by no means a fool, could not fail to observe this. Coupled with his antipathy for James, it made two excellent reasons for refusing to take him as a pupil, and to forbid him access to his painting room. The climax was reached when James made a copy of Morland's *The Travellers*, a picture that was in Ward's hands for engraving. Morland thought James' copy was his own work, a mistake that made him furious. He felt that he had nourished a rival who was as good a painter as himself. He feared to lose some of his laurels and their financial rewards, and could not face with equanimity the prospect of any loss of income. He always lived beyond what he could earn.

James plunged into painting with his usual impetuous enthusiasm, certain he had discovered a new phase of his genius, and a new road to fortune. This idea was no great mistake, though vain and self-glorious. It was a young man's dream that came true. The opposition and jealousy of his former hero only goaded him to greater efforts. A man of his character is always spurred on by opposition and finds profound satisfaction in overcoming real and imaginary obstacles.

George Raphael Ward, second son of James, writing *Artistic recollections of sixty years*, a copy of which I found among James' papers, admired his father, who won a reputation as an engraver remarkably quickly. The son said that James' services were soon in great demand by the popular portrait painters of the time. He engraved portraits by Opie, Owen, Sir William Beechey and others, and he worked no less hard and successfully as an engraver of historical subjects. Some of his most celebrated plates were *Diana and Nymphs*, after Rubens, and the *Centurian Cornelius sending his servant to Joppa*, after Rembrandt. Competent judges, unnamed, declared the latter to be one of the finest engravings ever executed in mezzotint.

This must have been some of the material that sold well in France, the market for which was closed by the Revolution. James believed the Revolution changed French taste in art as no doubt it did. English taste, too, was affected by this harrowing event. True taste turned to fashion, 'and which has increased ever since', wrote James sadly in 1847. He gave away his Rembrandt proof as well as Rubens and Billington. 'This left, I turned to painting anything that would pay best'; and in his choice of subjects he was influenced by Morland's example, by the love of domestic animals that had been so prettily displayed at Pratt's Bottom, and by the developing circumstances of the time.

CHAPTER III

The Landed Interest and its Artistic Tastes

Food production, the new name for farming, was the most important occupation of mankind before the Industrial Revolution, in England as in other countries. Most people had to farm because they were able to produce so small a net product, the surplus after they themselves and their animals were fed, that there was little to spare for people in other occupations. This was England's situation at Ward's birth; at the end of his long life industry was rapidly taking premier place in the national economy; imports by then were also helping the insufficient home production. When he was born the landed gentry ruled the country and their interest, in common with that of the rest of the community, was increased yields from the land. Not only would that make them richer because they could raise their rents, but it would provide a marketable surplus to feed the growing manufacturing population.

Ever since the Restoration of Charles II the interest of the aristocracy in agricultural improvement had been growing. It rose to fever heat at the end of the eighteenth century. 'Turnip' Townshend, the eponymous hero of the 4-course husbandry, had already gone to his place when Ward was born, but his efforts had left their mark. Only a year before Ward's birth Arthur Young made the first of the farming tours that were to make him famous, and to stimulate still greater enthusiasm for farming among the landed gentry and nobility who ruled the country.

Young flattered the landed proprietors in the preface to his *Six Weeks Tour through the Southern Counties of England and*

Wales that appeared in 1768. He said that 'those who suffer any improvement originally owing to *common* farmers are somewhat mistaken. All the well-known capital strokes of husbandry are traced accurately to gentlemen; from whence comes the introduction of Turnips in *England*? But from *Tull*. Who introduced clover? But *Sir Richard Weston*. Marling in Norfolk is owing to *Lord Townshend and Mr. Allen*. In a word the most noted improvements were devised and first practised by gentlemen; common husbandmen in a long period of years, imitate the method in proportion to the success, and so by slow degrees it becomes general.'

Young's first farming tour, an almost accidental investigation carried out in the course of a journey undertaken on other business, was designed to find out what improvements were being made in different places. They might be useful if adopted elsewhere. He was convinced that something good could be discovered almost everywhere. If it were possible to describe the good and valuable systems, and to interest the gentry who might be inclined to try them, an immense amount of good would result. His first work was so well received that in the next five years he travelled over nearly the whole of England and Wales and recorded what he saw in two further books, each of four volumes. The modest *Six Weeks Tour* only filled one.

Naturally Arthur Young visited the houses of the nobility and gentry on these tours and when he made shorter journeys later in life. They were the audience he wished to address and spur on; they would wish to see their own efforts described in his books; and they had the tradition of hospitality. Their number was comparatively small and though there were many strict graduations amongst them – a good deal of snobbishness if the truth were told – they formed a more or less homogenous group. He did not fail to describe the paintings that filled their galleries and the other luxuries with which they were surrounded.

They, too, formed the travelling public in the sense of travelling for pleasure or to visit relations, or to go to London, or one or other of the Wells. The great inns catered for them and their corteges. Some of the most wealthy noblemen and gentry travelled with the ladies in a coach, the gentlemen either on horseback or sitting with them. A following transport of servants and luggage included such luxuries as their own cook, provisions and wine, the whole being protected by a mounted guard of outriders. Such was the equipage of Sarah, Duchess of Marlborough. From this magnificence there was, of course, a descending scale to the individual gentleman travelling alone on horseback or in a post-chaise as Young did. Inns that catered for the wealthy were liable to be expensive and some of them, like the Angel at Cardiff, charged each person so much as a guinea a night, a large sum in those days, equal then to three weeks' wages of an agricultural labourer. The alternative was the hedge-ale house frequented by cattle and sheep drovers, itinerant tinkers, peddlers and gypsies, and all the other riff-raff of the eighteenth-century roads. An invitation to spend a night or more at the great house in the neighbourhood was all the more welcome to a man like Arthur Young. It was not despised by the traveller for pleasure, whose relations by blood and marriage were innumerable and widely scattered, and whose acquaintance through these relations and their friends extended pretty well throughout the whole of their class.

Young was very conscious of the need for pleasing the people to whom he wished to appeal. He was a wiser man than Ward who frequently quarrelled with them. Young was aware of the pride taken by the wealthy in conspicuous expenditure at all times in the history of the world. Conspicuous expenditure in his day took the form of building, of extravagant furniture, clothes and feasts, in collections of valuable jewels, libraries and pictures. The last were seen by the visitor because the proper place of pictures is on a wall. In some of the older families many of the pictures were ancestral portraits painted by Van Dyck and Lely, a just cause of pride. With his in-bred flair for pleasing Young inserted lists of the pictures he saw in great houses in his farming tours. This was a subject of immediate interest to his readers. By flattering such an interest Young was able to lead them on to what he had to say about farming.

The pictures then to be found in the galleries of the great

houses that Young visited were mainly of foreign schools; though several artists had painted animals, most usually race horses, and Sir Joshua Reynolds, Gainsborough and Romney were in their hey-day. It is not inappropriate that one of the first paintings Young remarked was at the seat of Lord Townshend at Rainham, Norfolk, the famous *Belisarius* by Salvator Rosa. Lady Townshend's dressing room was furnished with prints 'stuck with much taste on a green paper'. The pictures at Houghton, the celebrated seat of the Earl of Orford, had been catalogued by 'the very ingenious Horace Walpole,' so Young felt excused from giving a complete list. Guido, Rembrandt, Rubens, Titian, Poussin, Van Dyke are artists whose work was represented in this great house. Young's art criticism was limited to such expressions as 'amazing fine', 'poor' and were not illuminating; but, of course, it was only in this incidental way that he set himself up as an art critic, and perhaps only to demonstrate that his absorbing interest in farming did not detract from his general status of a cultured man. Lists of this kind are scattered throughout the three *Tours* published between 1768 and 1771.

Five years later Thomas William Coke entered upon his patrimonial estate at Holkham, Norfolk. At that time James Ward was still at bottle-washing or working in the vegetable shop. In 1778 Coke, inspired by the spirit of the age and perhaps by the writings of Arthur Young and the example of other Norfolk landlords, coupled with some small disappointment of political advancement, began improving his estate. This he made his life's work.

At first he was quite ignorant of farming. He did the sensible thing. He consulted the practical men he found in his neighbourhood. There were already some fine farmers in Norfolk, so he arranged a meeting of local men to discuss the burning agricultural questions of the day. Incidentally he got them to walk over his farm and tell him in their uninhibited Norfolk way what they thought of it. They were Norfolk farmers, wealthy, independent and plain spoken, so Coke obtained some good advice. Meetings of local men became annual events and developed into the great Holkham Sheep Shearing where hundreds of guests, landowners and farmers from all over the country, from far distant countries in Europe, and even from far off America were entertained in princely style for several days. New improved breeds of cattle and sheep were shown, and new inventions in implements. There were animated discussions of farms and methods of farming. This was a great undertaking for an individual landowner. Coke's reward was as great as his merit. By reason of the improved farming he was able to introduce on his estates, his rent roll rose it has been said, though this estimate has now been breathed upon, from £2,000 to £20,000 a year, a great sum at any time, but greater still when there was no income tax, and when a farm worker's wages were from 7/- to 9/- a week.

Coke was not alone in his efforts. Young's *Tours* describe the shining example of numerous great landowners. The Duke of Bedford had begun farming experiments at Woburn when Young visited the place in 1770. These experiments were to develop, and to lead to another great annual gathering, the Woburn Sheep Shearing. A similar event was arranged by the Earl of Egremont at Petworth in Sussex, and another in the beginning of the nineteenth century by John Christian Curwin at the Schoose Farm in Cumberland. John, fifteenth Lord Somerville, arranged one in London. These are only a few of the many. From the wilds of Northumberland to the rocky coasts of Cornwall the spirit of enterprise was beginning to excite the landed interest, and though it was slow in permeating to the whole body of farmers the yeast was stirring all over the country.

When the landed gentry were so absorbed in the pursuit of farming it was a happy conjunction for Ward that he was naturally drawn to the painting of animals. In this art he excelled. His success as an animal painter came later. His earliest painting, done in defiance of, and in imitative competition with Morland, was *Rustic Felicity*. He painted it in the first year he was out of his apprenticeship, almost immediately after Morland had refused to take him as a pupil. He sold this picture to J. Simpson of St. Paul's Churchyard, a famous publisher, who was so impressed that he ordered a companion piece, the *Rocking*

Horse, and gave James the job of engraving them both in mezzotint. These pictures are of well-to-do children, but their derivation from Morland's work is unmistakeable. James' next two pictures, *Compassionate Children*, and *Haymakers at Rest* were bought and engraved by his elder brother William, who published them. In these, too, Morland's influence is clear. Morland apparently did not resent this work for he collaborated with James in the production of a drawing book published by Simpson in 1793, each doing one half of the studies in the book.

Ward's early paintings are examples of a kind of picture that had developed from the stately portraits produced in the seventeenth and early eighteenth centuries. The innovation of the conversation piece, family group, or pictorial record of an event owed a great deal to Hogarth and his contemporaries. It was not, of course, a new thing. Hogarth too, in his moralities, painted a good deal of low life, very low life. He made the public familiar with pictures showing people at their everyday tasks as had the *London Cries* of an earlier date. Joseph Highmore, a contemporary of Morland, painted a series of pictures to illustrate *Pamela*, and also family groups. The younger Laroon and Philip Mercier depicted the aristocracy at their amusements, the former, for example, a *Concert at Montague House*, and the latter *A Family Party* engaged in a concert upon the lawn outside their mansion.

Following these came the great figures of Thomas Gainsborough and Sir Joshua Reynolds and their contemporaries. Both Gainsborough and Reynolds were country boys, as Ruskin, a scion of the nineteenth-century commercial class, somewhat scornfully remarked. Bred in country villages they learned there the country boy's reverential theory of the 'Squire'. To the end of their lives they painted the Squire and the Squire's Lady as the centre of the universe. Indeed in those days this admired class really was the centre of the English universe. Not only were they the central government in the House of Lords and House of Commons, but upon their country estates they ruled like princelings. When benevolent they were able to guide their tenants into the new paths that their efforts were so rapidly opening up to the agricultural interest. Besides this they could afford to have their portraits and the portraits of their families painted, and to buy pictures of the rural scenes that formed so large a part of their lives. The rural scene was not yet fashionable art, and Gainsborough found it almost impossible to sell the landscapes which were his first and most confirmed love. He painted portraits because it paid him handsomely to do so, but he painted rural scenes because it pleased him.

Gainsborough's famous and well known pictures, *The Market Cart*, *The Watering Place* and *Cornard Lane* are clearly fore-runners of Morland, who made such a success of selling this kind of production. Gainsborough died in 1778 before James Ward was out of time with his brother. He was born, or believed to have been born in Sudbury, Suffolk, a town to which he returned in 1745 after studying in London. Here he set up a studio and painted many local scenes. Seven years later he went to Ipswich where he again used the very attractive countryside as a venue for his work, the great skies and spaces of rural Suffolk being of commanding beauty. When he in turn lived there at the end of the century Constable believed that he could find Gains-borough reflected in all the landscape about the town.

East Anglia was the hub of all the farming improvements of the day. It was here that 'Turnip' Townshend had flourished at Rainham, and Coke of Norfolk was still carrying on the tradition of Holkham, during the whole of Ward's life. Lord Western, with whom he came into unfortunate contact in his latter years, led the way in Essex in the early decades of the nineteenth century.

Young was exploring the country houses of the great and famous just about when Ward was born. Already many portraits by Reynolds were in their galleries. Two portraits of the late Marquis of Tavistock and the reigning Duchess of Marlborough were in the yellow drawing room of the Duke of Bedford's house, Woburn Abbey. The Earl of Carlisle at Castle Howard, that vast and surprising edifice built by Vanbrugh nearly a century before, had one of himself. Young with solemn lack of humour remarked that the dog's head was very fine. At Hagley, Lord Littleton had hung his own pictures; at Kniveton the Duke of Leeds had the famous portrait of the Duchess. Young did not see any portrait by Gainsborough.

There were some landscapes, but the majority were sacred subjects by the old masters. Of the landscapes some were in Salvator Rosa's monstrous and terrifying style, some by the more recent French painters, Claude Lorraine and Poussin, were softer and more gentle. Amateurs, often members of the family, were proud of their own work in this style, and Young could hardly fail to descant upon their merits. The French painters were popular for two reasons. First the English nobility and gentry had always followed French fashions; second, they had developed a taste for travel in their own country. Besides doing the Grand Tour of Europe to complete their education many of the wealthy began to explore England. They went to Bath, to Harrogate, to Scarborough, and they found it interesting to see the country generally. They made tours into Cornwall, along the Thames, the Severn, and the Wye. They went to the Lakes and to Wales. This does not mean, of course, that the roads were as full of traffic as to a modern seaside resort on Sunday, but only that there was some travel. The population as a whole was no more than about a sixth of what it is today, and the number of those who could afford to travel was proportionately much less. These people saw 'scenery' and landscape. Their taste changed from one that enjoyed the horror of a scene where a terrified traveller was lost in a mountainous desert in a thunderstorm, to the smiling aspect of nature that made their travels enjoyable. Consequently they liked that aspect of nature in the pictures they bought.

Young reflects that change of taste in his appreciation of landscape. Like so many people today he found the Isle of Wight attractive. John Stevens of West Cowes lived in an agreeable seat on the rising ground near the sea. It commanded a noble view of the Channel from Portsmouth quite to Lymington and the mouth of the Southampton river. The high lands in Sussex, the hills in Hampshire and the woody coast of the New Forest bounded the view. One stroke of the eye saw the noblest river perhaps the world can exhibit, a beautiful expanse of water

scarcely ever free from the enlivening addition of all sorts of
ships from the largest men-of-war, down to some hundreds of
fishing boats. Young thought the Isle of Wight a most pleasant
spot to reside in. No place was happier in the beauties of a varied
country, hills, dales, mountains, rocks, wood and water, all in
perfection, a sea coast that had not a perch of flat land. They
scarcely knew what a marsh was. The land was admirably fertile
both in grass and corn and there was great plenty of game, particularly pheasants. The air was so healthy that there was not
one physician in the island.

Besides appreciating gentle landscape in the pictures they
bought the gentry tried to create it in their parks and gardens,
some of which were very extensive. The Duke of Bedford's park
at Woburn was ten miles round, a variety of hill and dale with
fine woods of oak. Young was driven by his noble host through
the woods towards the south. He looked up the great glade cut
through the park for several miles to catch a glimpse of a Chinese
temple at the other end. Further through the woods they came
to the Duchess' shrubbery, sixteen acres of land beautifully laid
out in the modern style of landscape gardening with many more
glorious oaks in it. There was an evergreen plantation created
from a rabbit warren, and a lake of about ten acres with an
island in the middle. On the island was a very elegant Chinese
temple large enough for thirty people to dine in. The kitchen,
where Lucullian feasts were prepared, was hidden in the
adjoining wood. This park was one of the largest in the kingdom.
Its walls enclosed some 3,500 acres, some of which yielded 'grass
good enough to fat large beasts'.

There were many such great parks, amongst them a vast one at
Castle Howard. Young, too, was impressed by the Duke of
Ancaster's park at Grimsthorpe through which the road passed
for three miles. Petworth Park is well known. There were many
more in the same or a lesser style of magnificence all over the
country. Very large sums of money were spent in taming nature
into the approved form. Lord Scarborough, for example, undertook to pay 'Capability' Brown, the great designer of the new form
of landscape garden, £3,000 for such work to be done at Sandbeck

in the county of York. This sum might be, if such an equation can be made, equal to at least £300,000 of our debased money.

Young's tours like Ward's travels at a slightly later date were made on horseback or in a post chaise. He had no choice. Horse transport was all there was. Travel was not easy, although a horse can walk almost anywhere. The roads were often ill defined so that a traveller on his way to Bath got lost between Reading and Newbury, something that is almost impossible to realise. The roads in the Sussex Weald were so heavy (they were only dirt tracks) that a noble lady who lived there habitually went to church in a carriage drawn by a team of oxen. These animals could drag the carriage through the mire better than horses. Almost everywhere the roads were little better than tracks, though across the wild spaces of the down between Winchester and Salisbury and like places were often a quarter of a mile wide. Every traveller went aside to avoid the ruts made by those who had gone before him.

Young's writings are full of complaints. Nevertheless people managed to travel. In the north between Preston and Wigan, Young traversed a turnpike road rutted four feet deep 'and floating with mud only from a wet summer'. In the sunken lanes of Essex his chaise had to be lifted into a field when he met a farmer's waggons; for otherwise it would have been impossible to pass. Where there is now an arterial road between Chepstow and Newport then it was a rocky lane 'full of hugeous stones as big as one's horse and abominable holes'. There was no wheeled traffic in Devonshire, only pack horses being used. It was nearly as bad in Wales. The roads in the Midland clay were almost impassable even in summer. Road making was not yet in its infancy. The art had died with the departure of the Romans and awaited McAdam to be reborn, though Ward has something peculiar to say about that, as will be seen later.

It was only natural that people who depended so much upon the horse as our ancestors should be intensely interested in their horseflesh. Their well-being depended upon it. They could not travel unless they had good horses either to ride or to pull their carriages. They could not hunt unless their stables contained fine

The Farrier's Shop

Sow and Piglets

Sheep in Barn

animals and hunting was the breath of life to the landed aristocracy of the eighteenth and nineteenth centuries.

The horseman is always competitive and our ancestors were
nothing if not gamblers. For more than a century Newmarket
had been flourishing as a racecourse where 'on a spacious heath,
several miles in length, the finest racecourse in the kingdom, a
scene of folly and vice, of reckless gambling and insane profanity,
was yearly enacted. Thither come the highest nobility and the
gentry of the kingdom to rub shoulders with cutpurses and pick
pockets, with sharpers and bullies, with jockeys and trainers, so
eager, so busy upon their wagers and bets that they seemed just
like so many horse coursers at Smithfield descending from their
high dignity and quality to picking one another's pockets,' was
the anathema of one by no means a puritan.

For the ordinary visitor not running his own horses Restoration Newmarket was tame enough. He was only a spectator looking on at the sport of the great landowners who ran the horses
that raced at Newmarket, York and Epsom. In Shadwell's
comedy *The True Widow* a character named Prig described the
day's round at that time. 'Newmarket's a rare place' he is made
to say, 'there a man's never idle; we make visits to horses and
talk to grooms, riders and cock keepers, and saunter in the heath
all the forenoon; then we dine, and never talk a word but of
dogs, cocks and horses, then we saunter into the heath again;
then to a cock match; then to a play in a barn; then to supper;
and never speak a word but of dogs, cocks and horses again; then
to the door porters' where you may play all night. Oh! tis a
heavenly life! We are never idle.' The scene on the heath was
painted by Peter Tilleman (1664–1734) and engraved on wood
by W. Babbage.

The owners naturally raced for the distinction of winning.
A winner gained great prestige amongst his compeers. Wagers,
too, were often so fantastically large that he made a profit, not
negligible even to the very rich, as well. Consequently the noble
or gentle owner of a successful racehorse was rightly very proud
of it; but the life of an animal is short, briefer even than that of
its owner. It passes away and nothing of it remains. It may win

C

a place in turf history where a line of writing tells its tale; or its portrait may be painted for remembrance just as its owner had his own portrait painted for the same reason. This is so obvious that as soon as racehorses became a hobby of the rich, a breed of horse painters appeared ready and willing to paint them. They were the aesthetic ancestors of part of James Ward's work, the portraits of famous racehorses and chargers, like Wellington's *Marengo* that he painted.

Peter Tilleman was one of these horse painters. He came from Antwerp and was first of all employed to make copies of famous paintings. He made nearly five hundred drawings for Bridges' *History of Northamptonshire*. These were of country houses and scenes as well as views of the small towns and villages that are now great centres of population. After this he readily obtained work from the landed proprietors making pictures 'of their country seats, hunting and racing scenes and portraits of their horses and dogs'. He was not the first artist to adopt these subjects, and this means of earning his living. He died thirty-five years before Ward was born, but his work demonstrates that the taste that enabled Ward to become a successful animal painter was not a novelty. Other painters in this genre were the Sartorius family which originated in Germany with the birth of John at Nuremburg in the year 1700. The greatest of them all was George Stubbs.

The nobility and gentry met some peculiar characters when they went to Newmarket and other race meetings. They mixed with the mob in the cock-pit, at the bull-baitings and other violent popular sports, just as their Regency descendants did in the same places and at the boxing ring. The classes were sufficiently distinct for these casual elbowings to be unimportant. They made for familiarity, but not for presumption. The lower orders did not forget their place and the upper classes certainly did not. This degree of familiarity did not reduce the haughty contempt of the ruling class for the mob, but did not make its antics absolutely distasteful. There was not the same fastidiousness that modern manners require. The personal habits of all classes were much alike. There was little hygiene though the lack of it was dis-

guised by velvets or silks among the wealthy and highborn, or
exposed in the ragged multitude. Poverty was looked upon as the
result of idleness and sin. Its appearance everywhere was
accepted as normal and irremediable. The people who were so
proud of their family portraits of men and women in fabulously
expensive clothes, surrounded by all the current apparatus of
wealth, of their grand paintings, of their costly animals, and of
gracious rustic conversation pieces, were equally ready to accept
the underworld depicted by Hogarth, possibly because the slums
of London were outside the boundaries of their exclusive environment.

Hogarth's work was one of the many influences that affected
George Morland. Just as he was influenced by the Dutch as well
as by Watteau and the contemporary French school, so he was by
the gentle rustics who adorned some of Gainsborough's paintings. Hogarth's influence was very moral and inspired the pairs
of pictures *The Idle Mechanic* and *The Industrious Mechanic*;
The Idle Laundress and *The Industrious Cottager*, part of
Morland's early work. The moral of these is as laudable as that
of Hogarth. They are pictures of humble people engaged in
homely or domestic occupations such as Morland loved to paint.
Similarly he loved to paint them in their easy moments sitting
outside or inside an inn, hurrahing at an ass race, setting out to
market or returning from it in the evening, weary and joyful, or
flushed and excited by 'a market glass'.

Many things were combining to provide a venue for James
Ward's peculiar talents. Interest in farming was being aroused
among the higher ranks of the landed gentry, who had formerly
been satisfied to draw their rents and spend them on pleasure and
sport. The lesser gentry, who lived on their small estates and
devoted themselves to hunting and shooting, were also becoming
interested. The taste for portraits of men and horses was expanding. The portraits of other animals, prize and even prized, were
wanted. The conversation piece that had developed out of the
portrait of a single person led the way to the narrative picture
of racing, shooting, hunting and so on to the modest events that
made up the lives of the humbler rural people. With the new

methods of farming the rich landowners were getting richer, and their ranks were soon to be joined by the new rich of industry. Their ambition was to buy land and become landed aristocracy, unmistakably merged in that class, their origins lost in oblivion. Some of these were, of course, yeoman or younger sons who had put their fortunes to the venture in trade or manufactory.

All the circumstances of the time combined to give the best of opportunities to James Ward, whose talents were exactly suited to the subjects wanted. If it is true that his apprenticeship to John Raphael Smith was only the result of an accidental vacancy that looked as if it had better prospects than bottle-washing, it was a happy accident indeed.

CHAPTER IV

Becoming a Painter

James Ward's star was certainly in the ascendant when his brother-in-law tried to dissuade him from painting and he refused to be advised. His combative disposition determined him to continue at all costs.

For about ten years he had lived in an environment that could not have been better for him if he had chosen it most carefully instead of being cast into it by chance. Opportunity was knocking at James' door, and though he was always more conscious of obstacles than opportunities, he worked like a slave to make himself capable of seizing it.

When he began painting Ward speedily became conscious of one thing that Morland, then his guide and envy, had not realised. A knowledge of anatomy is a help to a painter of animals and men. Here Morland has been accused of weakness. Ward determined to better him in that respect and entered John Brooke's School of Anatomy in Blenheim Street. There he learned to dissect animals and birds as well as human cadavers. His enthusiasm to learn was so warm that he often worked on alone in the dissecting room long after all the other students had left, in spite of his inability to control tremors of superstitious dread aroused by the companionship of corpses. His own words, quoted by Julia Frankau are, 'When I began with my predisposition to believe in Ghosts – early instilled and grown up with me – I felt a dread of being among Dead Bodies. The dissecting room was underground – filled with bodies and limbs and at one end an opening to a deep hole where the offal was thrown! When I began my operations (I believe the first day) a number of students were at work, and with them I felt more comfortable, but they left one by one as the morning advanced, and I was left quite alone! My eagerness in what I was about drew me to continue to twilight, when I began to feel a sort of dread come over me. At this moment I perceived in a very indistinct manner a strange form creep slowly up from the dark hole! Higher and higher and as it approached me I was about to utter a scream – when it spoke and proved to be a Bricklayer's Labourer, who had been all day engaged in repairing that dark chamber of putrid Bodies.' This gruesome and disturbing experience did not deter him from going on with his anatomical studies.

At the same time he realised that he would benefit by entering the newly formed Academy Schools; but it was not to be; he submitted a drawing from the antique as an entrance qualification. It was admired by Benjamin West and Northcote, who both complimented him upon it. Ward was flattered and thought himself certain to be accepted. Unfortunately the school was full and there was no immediate vacancy for Ward. He was told that he must wait six months and then submit another drawing. Quite naturally he was furious when he learned this. After being practically sure that he would enter the school at once, he was put off for six months. This alone was an incalculable insult to his gross pride, but in addition he was subjected to the ignominy of having to submit another drawing. His annoyance was pardonable, because he had been misled by the admiration West and Northcote had expressed for his work.

James Ward would wait for no one. He sent his drawing with another to the Society of Artists; but these works failed to receive the adulation he thought they deserved. This second set-back made him give up the idea of learning at school. He determined to teach himself, the hardest way in the world of learning anything. His certainty of his own powers drove him on, and no galley slave ever worked harder than he did in the early 1790's.

He worked all the hours of daylight, and cut his sleep to the minimum. The exhaustion induced was so severe that the noise of an alarum clock failed to rouse him. He therefore arranged to be awakened by a night watchman, who pulled a string hanging out of his bedroom window and tied to his wrist. Even this drastic expedient became ineffective because he untied the string in his sleep. At last he was reduced to fastening it to his ankle. This may be true; it is certainly romantic; and even if a fable, is an indication of the force that drove James Ward along the road of his destiny as if goaded by unresting demons. Some such method was employed by the knockers who roused the factory workers of the new industry from their brief hours of sleep.

Such assiduity and unremitting labour, though unguided by teachers of the traditional order, was bound to lead to some success. He gained it with the help of Simpson, and of his brother William Ward. It brought him to the verge of collapse, and he was forced to retire to his parent's cottage at Hendon. Fatigue from over-work was combined with melancholy. Ward was a disconsolate lover. Besides this emotional compensation, he conceived a passion for his cousin, Emma Ward, the daughter of his pious uncle William. To him, in his poverty, it seemed another hopeless passion. He had not been rejected, but his adolescent diffidence prevented him from declaring his love. Moreover he had to help maintain his parents, and his earnings were insufficient to keep a wife as well, a situation in which many young men have found themselves doubtless before, certainly since.

After about a year of this rustic seclusion Ward's indefatigable industry gained him success with *Rustic Felicity* and the other paintings already mentioned. This, with his engraving, enabled him to set up an establishment of his own, 20 Winchester Row, Paddington, with his sister Charlotte as housekeeper. Here he lived in some comfort, keeping a riding horse for convenience and pleasure like any other well-to-do young man, and employing several apprentices. He was well on his chosen road when the war with France broke out in 1793 and put a term to his market for engravings. This misfortune was compensated by Pitt's establishment in the same year of the semi-official Board of Agriculture, under the Presidency of Sir John Sinclair, Bart., with Arthur Young as Secretary. The effect of the first event was immediate; that of the second delayed, but eventually

advantageous to Ward. At the moment the setting up of the
Board confirmed and consolidated the interest of the landowning
class in the processes of farming and animal breeding. Increased
income was to be obtained by closer attention to their estates.
A more immediate and personal achievement was Ward's
appointment on New Year's day, 1794, as Painter and Engraver
to H.R.H. the Prince of Wales, an appointment that gave him
great social advantage.

The débâcle of the French market forced Ward to give up his
comfortable establishment though he had been immensely industrious just before, as he commonly was throughout his life.
He had exhibited no less than nine pictures at the Royal Academy,
and was occupied in mezzotinting eight or nine plates at the same
time. He was obliged to take lodgings in Bow Street, not a very
savoury neighbourhood then.

From these lodgings he issued forth to carry his pictures to the
dealers who naturally made the best of their market and paid
him trivial fees. Ward was naturally despondent at this wretched
turn of fate, but was not to be defeated.

In childhood he had been attracted by the consolations of
religion and in his young manhood he continued to seek them.
He became a regular and ardent follower of the ministry of the
Rev. John Newton. He attended all the Sunday services and
many of those held during the week.

Worry over his financial situation coupled with his failure to
make an immediate noise in the world, his excessive religiosity,
and the adoration of a penniless young man for a well-dowered
young woman, who moved in the fashionable world that was
quite inaccessible to him, was cause enough for mental unrest,
especially as Ward was not very stable in his mind. His overworked brain suffered something of a collapse; 'he became confused and irritable', and once more sought a refuge in the country.
This time it was a cottage on Hornsey Common, then an open
space surrounded by farms. From a point on Muswell Hill, the
south-east corner of Finchley Common, and another open space,
one admiring scribe said there was 'a most enchanting prospect
over Hornsey, Clapton, London, and the beautiful river Thames'.

With a judgement more profound than he could have realised he added, 'There are many points in this situation, that as much deserve to be adorned with elegant villas than any other spot in this, in many respects, highly favoured county' of Middlesex. The same view today is almost exclusively of houses, some of which hardly deserve to be called elegant villas.

Ward's cottage at Hornsey must have been surrounded by wild heath. Three fourths of the commons of the county were covered with furze and heath. It provided a little poor firing for the poor who lived nearby, or a trifle of feed for a few poor cattle, about enough to keep the animals from starving. Scattered gravel pits and stagnant ponds added to the picturesqueness of the place.

Commons like this afforded a chance to the enterprising poor to become squatters. They put up a wretched hovel of a shelter and unless driven off by the alert servants of the lord of the manor, gradually gained a foothold upon a tenement of sorts. They kept a few pigs and poultry that gained a scanty livelihood upon the scanty pasture. The best off amongst them might keep a cow. They would do casual jobs when they could get them, but there was a widespread suspicion that such characters, romantic as they looked in their rags and tatters on the painter's canvas, often eked out their honest earnings by petty thievery and dishonesty.

Another very serious evil was that the commons were the rendezvous of gypsies, strollers and other loose persons living under tents, characters that were later so vividly described by George Borrow. Some of these people had donkeys or horses, and some of them covered carts which answered the double purpose of concealing and carrying off the property they had stolen, and of a house for sleeping in at night. Their pilferings were, of course, mainly petty. They usually stayed a week or two at one place, and their animals were turned loose to pick up what they could about the tents. Any deficiency was made up from neighbouring haystacks, barns and granaries. The women and children begged and pilfered, told fortunes and sold trifles of their own manufacture, gathered wild fruit and so on; the men were horse

copers, chafferers, and practised all sorts of chicanery that became plain dishonesty when opportunity was favourable and
safe.

It was amongst such that Ward found many of his models.
Some of them may have sat for *The Gleaner's Return*, a picture
probably painted at that time as may be inferred from the hilly
character of its background of Hornsey scenery. During this
period of rustication Ward went on working hard, and, besides
engraving, he painted 'three fancy pictures for a gentleman in
Bethnal Green', but what these were he does not say.

Some financial stability restored health, and Ward's usual
imperfect state of mental balance must have been regained as a
result of this stay in the country. Encouraged, the young artist
returned to London and married his cousin. The wedding party
was held at his father's house in Kentish Town, to which he had
removed, and George Morland, between whom and Ward
friendship no longer existed, took advantage of the occasion to
play a rather unpleasant trick upon his brother-in-law.

The old marriage customs were then falling into disuse. One
was the butcher's serenade. Hogarth delineated it in his *Marriage
of the Industrious Apprentice*. The butcher's men, the bonny
boys that 'wore the sleeves of blue', when they learned of a
wedding party, jostled aside the regular musicians. With a very
present hope of beer to come they supplied a musical accompaniment to the festivity by clashing upon marrow bones with their
cleavers. Where only a small pourboire was to be anticipated this
band was made up of four, each man having his cleaver sharp-
ened so as to give out a different note; where the reward was expected to be greater eight bonny boys made up a complete
octave. If they were sufficiently skilful this series of notes would
have all the fine effects of a peal of bells. The butchers of Clare
Market had the highest reputation for their attainments on this
extraordinary dulcimer. Usually everything went off well. Both
musicians and wedding party accepted the serenade as a customary part of the rejoicing, and the butcher boys departed peace-
fully and sweetly enough after getting their fee in kind or in
money. The only break in the harmony that occasionally hap-

pened was a scuffle between the butcher's band and very insolent small boys who cast contempt upon their performance by rattling stones in tin cans. They had to be driven off with blows and contumely.

Morland carried the jest too far. Having arranged the butcher's serenade for his brother-in-law, whose growing skill he envied, and whose narrow puritanism annoyed him, he must have made them half drunk before the ceremony. Instead of performing outside the house they burst into it, and behaved with the most disgusting freedom, using the worst of oaths and offering violence to the guests who tried to put them out. This prank, if prank it can be called, in addition to George's continued dissipation, increased James' disgust with his brother-in-law. He resented strongly the suggestion then rapidly gaining currency, and not without some shadow of truth, that he was a pupil of Morland's or had modelled himself upon him.

This was a disadvantage because Morland's vogue was then on the wane, though a few decades later it was to rise, phoenix-like, from its ashes. Unscrupulous dealers made great play with the similarity of the two men's subject matter to reduce their buying prices. Ward's pictures were sold as Morland's, Morland's as Ward's, and confusion confounded. Ward's Academy picture *Selling Rabbits*, shown in 1795, was engraved by his brother. It was published in colour in 1796 with a companion piece by James, *The Citizens Retreat*, both were in the style of Morland's genius, the domestic scene in a rural setting he had made so much his own. The inevitable inference was made by the critics and dilettanti of the day. *The Bull Bait* exhibited in 1797 justified this general opinion. It was highly praised as Ward's first important picture, but John Raphael Smith rather maliciously asked James why he continued to imitate Morland. Ward himself declared that the subject was as rustic as Morland's work but wanted his vulgarity.

Smith added to his caveat against imitating Morland. He told James he was wise to give up mezzotinting because the market for tints was declining, and would soon vanish, an utterly mistaken prognostication. This fallacy may have confirmed James in the decision to make painting his future, although he was already recognised as one of the leading engravers in the country, a reputation achieved after his mezzotint of the *Douglas Children* was published in 1796. It was by engraving indeed that Ward continued to earn the major part of his living. He worked for Hoppner and others, as well as doing parts of mezzotints that were issued as the work of others, and whose provenance will now never be finally decided. The fate that Ward later resented bitterly was inevitable after 1797. In that year he exhibited two other paintings besides the *Bull Bait* at the Academy. They were *A Staffordshire Cow* and *A Staffordshire Bull*. Their success condemned him to be an animal painter of the highest order and the most unqualified recognition. He despised this magnificent achievement, misled perhaps by the theories of the grand style of painting that derived from Sir Joshua Reynold's lecture on that subject.

These two pictures are very early examples of a cattle breeder having the portraits of his favourite and outstanding beasts painted. They were the property of Mr. Thomas Princep of Croxhall. His estate was almost wholly in Derbyshire, but his cattle were of the long-horned breed, then in the highest favour by reason of Robert Bakewell's work in breeding them to a high degree of perfection at Dishley Grange in the neighbouring county of Leicester.

Throughout Staffordshire, a county where, owing to climate and soil, grazing and dairy farming were more important than arable farming, there had recently been some improvement in the cattle. This was the result of the good example of wealthy gentlemen in this county. They could afford to pay for prime stock. At the same time they could invest capital in improving their meadows and pastures so that their fine animals might have fine feed. One of them, Mr. Millar of Dunstall, thought that the gentry ought to keep fine bulls and boars, rams and stallions, for the use of their tenants, and thus ensure the grading up of all the stock in the county.

Princep, whose animals Ward painted, had brought his herd to a very high standard of perfection. The beasts were large, thick and well made, pretty good for the pail, and with a ready disposition to fatten early. His cows gave about eight quarts of good milk. Princep was satisfied that its high quality compensated for the larger output of inferior breeds. His bull 'Bright', kept for his own breeding only, was 'a majestic, noble animal; large, thick, heavy in the valuable points, with the least imaginable proportion of offal; with a skin handling soft and sleek'. He was so docile that three or four persons could handle him without his taking any notice, much less showing any signs of bullish ferocity. 'Bright Eye' his son, was three years old in 1794, a beautiful and most complete animal in the eyes of a breeder. William Pitt of Pendeford, a well known writer on farming, declared that he could not find a single fault in him. Such praise is rare indeed. It is no wonder that Princep wanted the virtues and beauties of his animals recorded pictorially.

Some of the animals were bred to large sizes. Lord Donegal of Fisherwick was another longhorn breeder who owned some stock from Princep's herd. One ox that he fattened was slaughtered in 1794, and gave 1,988 lb. of meat, 200 lb. of tallow, and 177 lb. hide. It sold for fifty guineas, a very high price. It compared favourably with a widely exhibited famous Lincolnshire Ox that was six feet four in height and weighed 2,800 lb. Another local ox from Leek, Staffordshire, weighed 2,369 lb. and a Scotch beast from the Island of Lewes in the Hebrides 2,423 lb. Other breeders in the neighbourhood were Lord Bagot at Blithfield, Sir Edward Littleton at Teddesley Park, Mr. Huskinson at Oxley near Wolverhampton, and of course Mr. Millar and Mr. Pitt himself (not to be confused with William Pitt the Younger, Prime Minister of England).

Several of the best animals, cattle, sheep and pigs belonging to these noble and gentle breeders were drawn. Engravings were made to illustrate William Pitt's *General View of the Agriculture of the County of Stafford*, a work that Pitt was engaged to do by the recently formed Board of Agriculture. Amongst these were Princep's bull 'Bright' and one of his cows. The drawings were made by E. Stringer of Litchfield and engraved by Neele of 352 Strand. Huskinson's cattle were painted by one Hughes.

This report, published in 1795, appeared before Ward's paintings were exhibited, but that is no reason why his Staffordshire Bull and Cow should not have been Princep's animals. He himself wrote a note on an etching that it depicted 'Bright', and was painted and etched by himself. *The General View of the Agriculture of Kent*, by John Boyes of Betteshanger, appeared in the same year. There are two engravings in this. One is a small Southdown ram belonging to Boyes which he drew. The other is a Kentish turnwrist plough hauled by four horses and attended by two men against an appropriate background. Both were engraved by Neele.

These books were part of a large scheme for a survey of the farming of the whole country, county by county, each prepared on a uniform plan. The idea was to collect all the possible information about the farming systems of the different counties and to publish it. Every farmer would then be able to study other people's methods, compare them with his own, and adopt any part that might seem valuable and useful.

The driving force behind the scheme was Sir John Sinclair, Bart., first President of the Board. Ward met him later on, and he influenced the painter's career as he influenced all with whom he came in contact. Like Ward, Sir John Sinclair was a man of indomitable energy and one abiding passion. Sir John's was the improvement of British farming, stimulated no doubt by his inheritance of a vast estate of 100,000 acres in the wilds of Northern Scotland. In appearance Sinclair was a great contrast to Ward. He was a man of gigantic stature and the undisturbed seriousness that so often accompanies this physique. He carried himself with a gravity and a sense of his own dignity that amounted to hauteur – his contemporaries of equal station were imperturbably convinced of their innate superiority to the rest of mankind. Sinclair was so completely lacking in humour that he could maintain his equanimity when placed in a ludicrous position because he failed to realise it. This defect enabled him to proceed with vigour in all his undertakings and to impress upon others the necessity for participating in his schemes, not because they were advocated by a great and powerful man, but because of their intrinsic value in the service of the nation. His individual collaborators were attracted by the prospects of large profits as well.

Legends always gather round such a man, and one of his achievements, when only eighteen years of age, has all the character of a legend. The family estates to which he had fallen heir a couple of years before were in the county of Caithness. Already he was active in improvements, but local communications were obstructed by a mountain, Ben Cheilt. There was no road over it. Everybody declared it impossible to build one. Not so the young Baronet! He surveyed the ground, lined out the road, ordered up the statute labour (six day's work on the country roads a year by the farmers and farm workers were a statutory obligation) fixed a date, and assembled a labour force of 1,260. Sinclair divided them into groups, each of which was given a space where the necessary tools and food was provided. He set them to work and the road was completed well enough to drive a carriage over it before night fell. This was an example of courage and determination likely to strike the imagination of a backward and remote country, and would be no mean achievement with modern equipment like bulldozers and so on. When performed with hand tools, pick, shovel, axe and hammer, it was stupendous.

This was the pace Sinclair set himself in his adolescence. He kept it up throughout his life. Amongst other activities sufficient to overwhelm an ordinary man, and certain in our less hardy age to bring on a nervous breakdown, Sinclair initiated and brought to completion *The Statistical Account of Scotland*. This was an economic enquiry on a scale never attempted before, and rarely since. It introduced a new word, 'Statistical' to our language, a little to our bane. The idea behind this enquiry was not original, but it had never before been conceived on such elaborate lines, nor carried to such a satisfactory conclusion, although similar and more limited enquiries had been made by Sir Robert Gordon, Sir Robert Sibbald, Walter Mcfarland Maitland, Dr. Webster and Pennant.

Sinclair had the idea that he could do the same sort of thing in England and Wales, but found it impossible without official backing. This led to the publication of his *Plan for establishing a Board of Agriculture* in 1793. It was immediately challenged by William Marshall, a Yorkshireman, who had returned home to commence farming after a financially successful sojourn abroad.

Marshall had already begun his one man survey of the *Rural Economy* of England and claimed that the idea of a Board of Agriculture was originally his own, more particularly the proposals to make a national farming survey. Sinclair roundly said the idea had not been borrowed from anyone. It was not even new. The Royal Society had tried to make a similar survey as long before as the reign of Charles II. He did not think it could be successfully made unless a Board of Agriculture was set up. Consequently he came to London in 1792 resolved to accomplish this object or to retire to his estate for good. He did not fail. William Pitt the Younger, then Prime Minister, supported him with a modest grant from the government.

Young might himself have laid some claim to have shown the practical way to make agricultural surveys. He had begun the records of his farming tours so long before as 1768, and it was a pamphlet he issued after making his *Tour in France* in the early days of the Revolution that secured the appointment for him. *The Example of France* greatly pleased the aristocratic ruling class who feared that example might be followed in England.

When appointed Secretary to the Board Young was obliged to give up a grandiose scheme of land reclamation on the Yorkshire Moors. He did so reluctantly, but probably saved his money. He complained, too, that residence in London left him little time to manage his farm at Bradfield Hall, Suffolk. Indeed he was full of complaints.

As president of the new Board of Agriculture Sinclair insisted that the first business to be done was to make a national survey of farming. He at once made arrangements for the preparation of surveys, county by county. Of these William Pitt's *Stafford* and John Boyes' *Kent* are examples.

This infuriated William Marshall whose own personal survey

was already advancing. His *Rural Economy of Norfolk* was published in 1787. His plan, too, was more modern than the official one. His survey was regional. Though he did it all himself he completed his self-imposed task long before the Board's series of county surveys. He had hoped for some appointment on the Board and was bitterly disappointed, even infuriated, when Young became Secretary.

Young himself was no less frank a critic of Sinclair. He professed himself disgusted at the casual way in which the President selected persons to prepare the Board's draft reports upon the different counties. Some men were employed who hardly knew the right end of a plough. One was an unemployed half-pay officer who wanted a summer excursion. Most of these people were chosen by Sinclair before the first meeting of the Board, a procedure highly improper.

In spite of the personal dissensions of its officers the initial work of the Board progressed rapidly. The first draft reports made by those unsatisfactorily appointed reporters were printed, circulated amongst the gentry and farmers of the respective counties, and resurveyed in the light of their criticisms; but the corrected editions were produced only slowly. Two of the earliest were William Pitt's and John Boyes'. Not for a few years was James Ward to meet Sir John Sinclair, but the inclusion of portraits of livestock in these works must have helped stimulate the fashion for such pictures that opened an avenue of progress and profit to James Ward and other artists.

At this time Ward was excessively busy. He was engraving, and also painting and exhibiting at the Royal Academy. Unfortunately the long series of disputes that marred his life began. He had an obscure quarrel with Hoppner about a print, a portrait of Mrs. Taylor that was suppressed. Nevertheless he engraved Hoppner's portraits of Admiral Duncan, and one of John Ravoult after Beechey. Both were published in 1799. In that year he showed *The Lion and Tiger fighting* and an *Alderney Cow* at the Academy.

Hopeless confusion reigns over the stories told by his three modern biographers about the next few years of Ward's progress, not to speak of the confused and involved stories disclosed in the correspondence of his embittered old age. Gilbey says that the *Alderney Cow* was probably painted for Sir John Sinclair, and Grundy says that it was probably part of the Boydell Works, of which more anon; Julia Frankau is always vague about dates, and Ward's correspondence does little to untangle this skein. Miss Frankau puts the date of Ward's meeting with Sinclair at 1804.

Ward was prosperous enough in 1799 to move from Lisson Grove to Newman Street, a turning off Oxford Street. This house was commodious enough for large dinner parties. To these he invited patrons and acquaintances amongst the aristocracy. A large studio had been built over the stables, suitable both for painting and as an exhibition room. Ward was one of the first artists to move into Newman Street, afterwards a colony inhabited by painters and engravers. Benjamin West, President of the Royal Academy, was a neighbour. The two men, both of whom often worked far into the night, would, in friendly competition, take note of the time when the other put out his light.

It was in 1799 too, that Ward entered into partnership with his brother and Sir William Beechey. In Beechey's picture *The Review* he painted the King's favourite charger 'Adonis', that ridden by the Prince of Wales, and some ridden by the generals. The partnership included a Dr. Daw, who helped to finance James' undertaking of engraving *The Review*. This enterprise was financially successful. It encouraged his brother William to offer him a partnership, or to join the other two in setting up a publishing business at the premises in Newman Street. William was not doing too well at this time, and agreed that James should paint or engrave just as he wished.

The new firm was launched with great éclat and the largest anticipation of success. Pictures by Opie and other well-known artists were bought, and a new printing press installed. James threw himself with whole-hearted enthusiasm into the project. He painted pictures, he engraved his own, and those bought for the purpose. Besides painting his output of engravings was larger than that of his brother, and he did his best, though he was not himself a talented business man, to supply the defects of the firm's manager, Dr. Daw.

James took a rosy view of the firm's prospects, but did nothing to help them by quarrelling with Copley in the year it was founded. The dispute was about some work and is highly characteristic of Ward. It shows how difficult he must have been to deal with. The job was a private one in the sense that it was not to be done as part of James' work for the newly-formed firm. Copley had made a large painting, entitled *Lord Duncan's victory over the Dutch*, of the surrender of the Dutch Admiral de Winter to Lord Duncan on board the *Vulnerable*. Ward agreed to make a mezzotint of this picture in his best and most finished manner, the engraving to be finished by the following April. Ward was to be paid 125 guineas when the first proof was taken, and a second similar amount when four hundred impressions were completely finished. But another etching was asked for at the same time, and James tried to do the two jobs at once. Then he fell ill and so the work was not completed until June. This was James' fault and misfortune combined. When it was finished Copley was short of funds, and could not pay the first instalment promptly.

Neither party would admit any failure to fulfil the terms of the contract and a long and acrimonious correspondence ensued. In his letters Ward repeated his version of the affair *ad nauseam* as he always did, when so deeply impressed by his own statement of the facts. He was continually engaged in disputes, and made a practice of preserving a pugnacious letter he thought it necessary to pummel anyone with. His surviving correspondence is consequently bulky with letters about the same subject. The difference with Copley was finally resolved, and the two men's pleasant relations happily restored.

It may have been at this time that Ward made an attempt to gain the official recognition that his work certainly deserved by becoming an Academician. Whatever the exact date, the circumstances are well known. Ward had now been a painter for several years, and he wanted recognition by the Royal Academy. This he could not secure if he entered that august circle as an associate engraver. An associate engraver must remain an associate; he could never be an R.A. James accordingly put up as a painter. This may have been resented by those artists whose pictures he had engraved, and all the more because the pictures he had shown at the 1798 exhibition had earned him the title of 'The English Paul Potter', the famous Dutch painter who specialised in pictures of livestock.

Hoppner called upon Ward's wife to persuade her to discourage him from painting. He told her that as an engraver James had done something that had never been done before. All the reputable artists of the day wished him to continue to engrave their works. By doing so he would command everything and make a fortune, the aim of every reasonable person, which when obtained left nothing else to wish for. By persisting in trying to become a painter at his time of life (he was then thirty years of age at least) he was indulging in folly because he could never expect to overtake and compete with the established painters. The only result would be the loss of the best engraver of the day which Hoppner said, 'we want, and the gain of a painter which we do not want'! Hoppner and other painters accordingly voted against him, and his election continued to be opposed for some years.

Not altogether unreasonably and entirely concordant with his disposition this opposition only confirmed James in his determination to shine as a painter. When his wife told him about Hoppner's call he said 'Does Hoppner think so? Then I will try. I shall engrave no more', but, of course, he could not afford to throw his living away. During the next seven years he mezzotinted a good many pictures including Hoppner's portrait of Lady Heathcote.

This did not change his determination. He used engraving as a pot boiler while he endeavoured to establish his reputation as a painter. His 1798 Academy picture gained him the label 'The English Paul Potter' as already mentioned. This, of course, placed James in the category of animal or cattle painter, something he hated but excelled in and tried so hard to escape. Potter was a seventeenth century painter of the Dutch School which was so much condemned by Ruskin for its realism. Sneeringly he wrote of the school, 'Our only idol glitters in the shape of a pink

pot and all the increase offered thereto comes out of a small
censor or bowl at the end of a pipe. Of deities and angels, prin-
cipalities and powers, in the name of our ditches let us have no
more. Let us have cattle and market vegetables.' There was, he
said, no true humanity in this rural feeling, and indeed no feeling for beauty. No incident was painted for the sake of the incident, a remark that is rather inexplicable. Did James in a
prophetic moment foresee this scathing criticism by a pundit
of the Victorian age, well into which he lived, and shrank from
being included in such condemnation? Paul Potter was the best
painter of herds and cattle, but, in Ruskin's opinion, did not
even care for sheep, only for wool, nor for cattle, but only horns,
as if to condemn him for being an artist occupied with the
appearance of things, surely the proper business of an artist.

Was it in the same year 1799 that Ward's resented fate was
practically sealed by the casual chance of his having visited the
Isle of Thanet? He may have gone there in consequence of having
published *A View of Kingsgate in the Isle of Thanet*, a painting
by George Walker. Whatever the reason, it was in the Isle of
Thanet that he made the acquaintance of Sir John Sinclair.
Sinclair's interest must have been largely taken up with the
splendid farming of the Isle where there was already some market
gardening for the supply of London: spinach, kidney beans and
peas being grown, and radish seed carefully cultivated, as well
as cress and white mustard. Heavy yields of cereals were obtained on the excellent soil of the Isle, and light implements were
used by the enlightened farmers who found them economical
and practical. When Sinclair met Ward he gave him a commission to paint a cow. Ward himself in a note made in his old
age described the animal as a 'high bred' cow, but Sir Walter
Gilbey said it was an Alderney Cow; Grundy that it was a Dutch
cow. Whatever the breed, the painting gave Sinclair great satisfaction. Ward got all the introductions to noble breeders that he
could possibly cope with, and received all the jobs of painting
animal portraits that he could possibly do. Once again chance
played a part in Ward's destiny. This meeting largely determined
his future.

CHAPTER V

The Boydell Business and Progress to Waterloo

The mystery of Ward's chronology deepens here. If James met Sir John Sinclair in the Isle of Thanet in 1799, Sir John was then under a temporary eclipse. At an election in 1798 he had been ousted from the Presidency of the Board of Agriculture by John, fifteenth Lord Somerville, who had only a majority of one vote, 13 over 12.

The picture that Ward painted for Sinclair is said by Grundy to have been for the Board of Agriculture, and not a private commission. Grundy had also seen a copy of an engraving of *Bright, the Staffordshire Bull*, on which Ward had written 'for the Board of Agriculture and etched by James Ward'.

The fashion for animal portraits was now well established. Ward painted and engraved *Ewe of the Leicestershire Stock*, shown by the Duke of Bedford at Smithfield in 1799, the print being published the following February. This painting was made for the Duke. It had no official implication, but is a clear pointer to Ward's growing fame as an animal painter, and his acceptance by the leaders of the nation, both social and agricultural.

Early in 1800 another engraving was issued that reflects Ward's rise. It was a portrait of Lord Somerville, after Woodforde. His Lordship was dressed in his uniform as Colonel of the Somerset Yeomanry, a regiment raised on his own estate and commanded by him.

Somerville had been elected President of the Board of Agriculture to restrain the flood of printing organised by Sinclair. The Board's finances were in parlous case when he took over. The cast of his mind was very different from Sinclair's. He was a practical farmer rather than a politician, and though he wrote a book and some slighter contributions he was not so completely under the spell of a passion for collecting information. Nor was he ambitious for public recognition.

Before his election his career was quite orthodox. Born in 1765 he was educated at Harrow, then for three years under a tutor at Peterborough, whence he entered St. John's College, Cambridge, taking his M.A. in 1785. The fashion was to proceed from the University upon the Grand Tour, and during his travels Lord Somerville met Francis, Duke of Bedford. The two noblemen, who were both greatly interested in farming, and played prominent parts in its development, joined forces to complete their tour.

On his return home Somerville was confronted with difficulties. The Somerset property was thrown into Chancery and for six years he was allowed to occupy only one farm of poor hill land. His assiduity and up to date methods turned it into a productive property, paying 11 per cent on the capital invested. This time of trial ended when his other estates were restored to him, but it was not till 1796 that he succeeded to the barony as fifteenth lord of the whole patrimony of English and Scottish estates.

A year before he had become a yeomanry officer in the face of the threat of a French invasion. At the same time he set out his creed in a pamphlet, *A Short Address to the Yeomanry of England and others*, 1795. This told the yeomen that they had a right to be proud of their profession as farmers particularly when the first men in the country were anxious to learn it as a trade, and women, not the old ones who had nothing else to do, but young women who possessed all that wealth and splendour of fashion could give, were studying farming as a science. The King himself was applying every leisure moment to agriculture.

Somerville's Presidency of the Board only lasted till June, 1799. He was also President of the Bath and West Society for 1798. He was an original member of the Smithfield Club, and its Vice President from 1814 to 1819. His appointment as Lord of the King's Bedchamber in 1799 brought him into close relations

with His Majesty, closer indeed than these two enthusiast
farmers had been, although in 1798 they held a ploughing match
between Somerville's double-furrow plough drawn by four oxen
and the King's single-furrow plough with six oxen. Somerville
won by a handsome margin.

A royal ploughing match was something new in the country,
and must have attracted a great deal of attention; but ploughing
matches were not themselves new. They had long formed one
of the usual competitions at the meetings of local agricultural
societies whose prizes of money to the ploughman and silver plate
to the farmer were not uncommon.

The King was a shining example to his subjects, not only by
participating in this famous ploughing match, but also by the
vast amount of work he had done reclaiming the wastes of
Windsor Great Park. Arthur Young was the greatest of the many
publicists concerned with the nation's farming, but the head of
the reigning house must have been superior to him in the extent
of his influence, and his position as head of the state was even
more impressive in an aristocratic society than Young's indefatigable writing, talking and travelling.

Windsor Castle was run like a farmhouse, and the Park as a
farm. A strict and frugal routine was followed, early to bed and
early to rise, meals of no pretence to regal splendour, but solid
food from his own farm and fixed rules for passing the day. His
sons who did not share their father's tastes, but were of a different
stripe, as the Regency and their reigns show, fled the place in
dismay.

No circumstances could have been more propitious for a
painter of Ward's capacity. He had already been 'Painter and
Engraver to H.R.H. the Prince of Wales' for some years. He
added to his reputation by his paintings and engravings of Princep's cattle, he had carried out a successful job for Sir John
Sinclair, he had painted the King's charger in Beechey's *Review*
and he had engraved Woodforde's portrait of Lord Somerville,
not to speak of delightful paintings like *Rural Felicity*.

It was no wonder that when a scheme for making a series of
paintings of scale accuracy to record the different breeds of live-

stock in the country was planned, Ward, already the foremost animal painter of his day, should be chosen to do the work.

Precisely when or by whom the scheme was originated is another darkling mystery. It is said to have been planned under the auspices of the Board of Agriculture, and from Ward's holograph note on an engraving of Princep's bull, it appears that he did work for the Board. Certainly the project was one in which Somerville was concerned, though whether as a member of the Board or as a private individual it is impossible to say. Sir John Sinclair, too, was most probably a participant, if only to the extent of having ordered an animal painting from Ward. The extant records of the Board, now in the keeping of the Royal Agricultural Society of England, disclose nothing of their interest. *

The management and finance of the scheme was put in the hands of the great firm of pictorial publishers, Boydell and Co., to whose illustrated Shakespeare so many fine artists of the day contributed. This firm was famous for some of the illustrated topographical works then so popular.

The scheme was on the grandiose scale customary amongst its backers. Ward was to paint a full collection of portraits of the significant breeds of cattle, sheep and pigs. It was expected to amount to some two hundred works, all of which were to be photographic in manner, and drawn to precise scale of measurement and proportion in the selected animals. Boydells agreed to pay fifteen guineas for each subject, and to supply sums for Ward's expenses in travelling about the country to see the animals he was required to portray. Ward expected to deliver one picture a week and that Boydells would pay him at once, so earning a regular and substantial income. This was not Boydell's idea. James had no money of his own and relied upon his earnings for his livelihood. Without payment for his work he in turn could not pay his daily expenses. For a man of his strict morals this must have been very galling. A long dispute ensued, and gave James just cause for complaint.

* The late Capt. E. H. Gregory, who died more than 40 years ago but was at one time the Society's Librarian, examined these papers and could find only two letters to Boydell of no significance.

This work was begun, so far as can now be ascertained, in 1801. A list of subjects had been drawn up by Lord Somerville, assisted by Mr. Lawrenson. James, in a later diatribe about the whole business, described how he went to Plaistow and various other parts of London and its neighbourhood to butchers and others after prize cattle. When he found them he had to paint them by the guttering light of torches, working all night because the beasts had to be slaughtered in the morning. He spent at least three weeks in that way, and his resentment at working in such conditions was natural. The bad light made the work difficult. Having to do it at night prevented James from indulging a passion for dancing that his wife, that toast at Almacks, most assuredly shared.

James' reputation and acquaintance amongst the great and fashionable led them both into extravagances. In spite of his rapidly growing income, even when bolstered by the Boydell contract, he found it difficult to meet his expenses.

The Wards' life was full of incongruities. The splendour of the evening entertainments were a great contrast to the personal visits of Mrs. Ward to Covent Garden market at six o'clock in the morning. At the market she chaffered and bargained for supplies of carefully selected vegetables and fruit. She carried the goods home in her shopping basket, or it was carried in stately circumstances by an attendant footman in uniform. James' uncomfortable efforts to make pictures at night in gloomy cowhouses lit only by flickering torches were unknown to those who gathered round his dining table gleaming with silver and white napery, and lit by a multitude of candles. His wife's marketing exploits at dawn were equally unknown to the beaux and dandies who gathered round her at Almacks, where she displayed her much adorned beauty and elegance.

The year 1801 was occupied with the Boydell business. James had been supplied with a second-hand gig by the firm, but they did not fail to charge him for it. The price of £27 was not extravagant, but proved a sorry bargain. The unavoidable rough usage of continual travel over poor roads and into the remote countryside would have been a severe strain on a new vehicle;

it was altogether too much for an old one. Having spent a lot of money on occasional repairs James was forced to abandon it in Wales when it finally collapsed in the following year.

The first journey James made was to Brighton and Lewes to visit Mr. Ellman. This farmer was a great breeder of Sussex cattle but is better known as the first man to develop Southdown sheep. Ellman's sheep were as famous as Bakewell's cattle, and when Ward visited him were already spreading to parts of the country far from their original home.

John Ellman of Glynde succeeded to his father's farm in 1780, and occupied it for more than fifty years. He told Arthur Young that he had spent more time at the plough handles than at a grammar school, his father having allowed him to attend school only during two winter quarters. The Sussex Downs at that time were covered with their own special breed of sheep. A stretch six miles wide and thirty-three miles long lay between Bourne and Steyning. It carried some 200,000 ewes, and the whole tract was believed to feed one and a half sheep to the acre.

Ellman farmed 580 acres, and at one of his harvest homes he entertained upwards of eighty men, women and children. For the feast he provided fifteen or sixteen stones of beef, six or eight stones of mutton, besides more than one hundred of plum pudding, forty or fifty gallons of strong beer and bread in proportion. The fragments that remained after the feast were distributed among the poor of the parish.

The fame of Ellman's Southdowns, like the sheep themselves, spread through the land, and even abroad, and the enthusiasm of their adherents knew no bounds. In 1798 the Emperor of all the Russias ordered two of Ellman's rams through His Majesty George III. The Duke of Bedford set their price at three hundred guineas for the two, and himself took two at the same price, declaring himself well satisfied with his bargain.

This was not Ellman's first acquaintance with the Duke, who was associated with him and Mr. Astley in the foundation of the Smithfield Club, 1798. The Duke was a frequent visitor at Glynde. His arrival might well have been dreaded. The farmer's family would have feared a fastidious peer not satisfied with less than palace accommodation, but in fact the Duke was welcomed with unruffled pleasure by everyone in the house. His Grace possessed real simplicity of character, and was quite content with the normal arrangements of the household. He accepted them all with the suavity of perfect courtesy.

There has rarely been a time in our history when class distinctions were more severely defined or the carriage of the more superior classes more haughty. A farmer like Ellman, whose work had won him high recognition freely and graciously accorded, had his own measure of self respect. He corresponded with many of the nobility who were interested in farming. Correspondence between intimates of the same class was then carried on with a formality that is foreign to the modern slangy scrawl, but much of this correspondence is informed with a very real admiration on one side, and a perfect comprehension of his own value on the other.

Lord Somerville was a lifelong friend. He introduced Ellman to the King in 1799. Somerville's invitation to Ellman was couched in deferential terms. 'Would it suit you,' he wrote, 'to be up by Thursday which is the day the King looks at his farm at Kew. I wish to make you known to him and for this plain reason, that our trade has not many of your complexion to boast of.' Naturally Ellman regarded this as a Royal Command and 'Farmer' George received him at Kew. They had a fine lengthy talk. The King had recently received his gift of Merino sheep. He gave Ellman ten ewes and two rams, but the great Sussex farmer was not to be persuaded to abandon the breed of his native hills.

Though always remembered and to be remembered for his work in perfecting the breed of Southdown sheep, John Ellman worked on the beautiful Sussex Red Cattle as well, and won many prizes with them. His friendship with Lord Somerville was a good and sufficient reason for Ward to be sent to him to paint examples of his cattle and sheep. Living in the inaccessible wilds of Sussex, more acquainted with the plough handles than his book, yet the friend of many of the nobility and gentry, Ellman was rather like Ward. He had never lived in the festering slums surrounding Thames Street, but Ellman's childhood was extremely austere. He learned his farming by doing it; he worked long hours for little reward as a farmer's son employed on the family holding so often does. Both had risen from their humble beginnings to the foremost place in the profession they followed; both were puritanical in an age when riot, drunkenness, gambling and folly of all sorts flourished like a green bay tree, though these self-indulgent men were engaged in fighting a terrible war, and at the same time leading the development of the country's resources. Meeting Ellman, a man of whom even he must have approved, was an auspicious opening to Ward's travels in search of prime animals to paint.

His next journey to Windsor Castle was equally pleasant. He went there to paint two of the King's sheep. Permission to do this must have been highly flattering to Ward, and gratifying to his taste for high society. Ward's papers disclose no very great interest in and little knowledge of farming, so he was not at all the sort of talker the King would have liked to listen to. He was already slenderly acquainted with the King, but probably had no opportunity of becoming more closely acquainted with His Majesty at Windsor where he spent a week. These two short journeys over, Ward set out on tour of the southwest, through Dorset, Devon, Cornwall, Somerset, Wilts and Berkshire, travels that occupied some two months. There were various renowned breeds of animals in these counties; the Dorset Horn sheep, the Red Devon cows that spread from the borders of Dorset across North Devon into Cornwall and Somerset, the Wiltshire sheep and the Dorset pigs. There was nothing outstanding about Cornish beasts, though Ward may have found some examples of the so-called French cattle there. These came from the Channel Islands and the coast of Normandy, and were the forebears of the now famous Jersey, Guernsey and Alderney cattle.

Ward painted at least four Devonshire cattle. These may have been the originals of the engravings that illustrate Charles Vancouver's *General View of the agriculture of the County of Devon*, 1808, another of the Board of Agriculture's County Surveys. He painted an Isle of Portland sheep, a smaller and more agile variety of the Dorset; a South Devon ewe; a Devonshire hog; a Berkshire boar, hog, pig and sow separately; Chinese boars and sows then used for crossing with native breeds all over the kingdom. Possibly he painted others that are not closely enough identified with the titles to show just where Ward found his animal models.

On his return Ward visited his patron and friend the Duke of Bedford, who had supplied him with many letters of introduction to facilitate Ward's work for the Board of Agriculture. The purpose of Ward's visit was to paint 'only one sheep' as he somewhat disparagingly remarks. If his visit coincided with the annual sheep-shearing at Woburn it could not have been other than enjoyable, particularly to a man like Ward who burgeoned in an atmosphere of titles and dignitaries.

Francis, fifth Duke of Bedford, like the King, established a private experimental farm at Woburn Abbey. It was one of those enterprises that did so much for English agriculture; it has now become an official appendage to Rothamsted Experimental Station, another undertaking that was started by a private gentleman, Sir John Benet Lawes, at a later date.

The Duke, following the example of his friend, Coke of Holkham, instituted an annual sheep-shearing at Woburn. Here the different breeds of sheep were shown. Prizes were given and rams were let. New and old types of implements were displayed. There was an incalculable spate of good talk amongst the assembled company. In 1801 this show was attended by hundreds of agriculturalists and breeders from all over the country and lasted four days.

On the first day, Monday 16th June, 1801, a public breakfast was given by the Duke at 9 a.m., but long before this, even before the break of day, the roads to the Abbey were choked with traffic. Many of the farmers who could find no conveyance must trudge along the unmade roads of English midsummer. At 11 a.m. a royalty arrived, attended by Sir George Osborne of Chacksands, at whose home he was staying. Soon after the company, numbering some hundreds, proceeded in a grand cavalcade to the new farmyard in the park to inspect the sheep-shearing. Certificates were given by His Grace. The ewes were inspected, and the tups for hire examined by attentive and exacting hirers to be.

The Duke, who wanted the better breeds of sheep introduced into Bedfordshire, had offered a prize of fifty guineas to the farmer who should have spent the largest sum on New Leicester or Southdown ewes between June, 1799, and Christmas, but the winner was not announced. An original entertainment was provided by the cattle modeller, George Garrard, who exhibited a model of a piece of the loin of Mr. Smith's three shear wether that had won the premium in 1799. The fat was seven inches thick. It would not be much to modern taste. Garrard might very well have been a rival of Ward in the business of animal painting had not his taste diverted him to sculpture. His artistic life began when in 1781 he exhibited some pictures of horses and dogs. He had been a pupil of Sawray Gilpin at the Royal Academy Schools. Sir Joshua Reynolds became interested in his work on seeing his *Sheep Shearing at Aston Clinton, Bucks.*, in 1793.

Two years later Garrard began to make models of cattle for the use of landscape painters. There was then no copyright in such things. Garrard petitioned Parliament and secured an Act to supply this defect. This gave designers copyright in all new models for sculpture, an immense benefit to the profession generally, as well as a great advantage to himself. Its provisions assured him of getting paid for the right of disposing of the casts from which his own models were produced. The Royal Academy congratulated him upon this achievement.

His work of producing scale models of cattle led him to believe that the published paintings and engravings of livestock were poor representations. His own scale models could be sent, he argued, to foreign countries to encourage them to buy British cattle, and would be a record for comparison with future development. They were made from the best specimens selected under the instructions of the Duke of Bedford and the Earl of Egremont. As a corollary to the models he issued an illustrated book, *A description of the different varieties of oxen in the British Isles with coloured engravings on an exact scale from nature*, under the patronage of the Board of Agriculture, which was printed for the author by J. Smeeton, London, 1800, a folio that cost five guineas with uncoloured plates or ten guineas with coloured.

Garrard did not include all the breeds, but provided twelve pictures that he afterwards added to. They were Devon, Hereford, Leicester, Sussex, Holderness, Yorkshire Polled, Suffolk Polled, South Wales or Pembroke, North Wales or Anglesey, Scotch, Irish and Alderney. He substantiated the accuracy of his plates and models by reference to their origin. Mr. Conyers of Epping recommended a lot of twenty-four Devon heifers and two bulls he had bought for use in making Epping butter. Mr. Lechmere of Rydde near Worcester described Herefords for him; and Tully of Hunterton, a good breeder, helped. One of Tully's beasts won the Smithfield prize in 1799 and was sold for £100 to a Reading butcher. William Pitt of Pendeford, author of several county reports, including the *Stafford* that may well be illustrated by Ward's Staffordshire Bull and Cow, described the Longhorn for Garrard. A correct model of a Smithfield prize-winning Sussex beast was placed in a museum at Petworth. The specimen of the Holderness breed shown was taken from His Majesty's stock at Windsor, and may have been given to the King by Sir Joseph Banks.

Plainly Garrard had much the same kind of support for his work on cattle as Ward. He was similarly welcomed at Woburn by his patron the Duke of Bedford. At the sheep-shearing he exhibited his models in the hope of selling specimens. He did a self-portrait engaged in this business when the Duke, encouraged by the success of Garrard's early painting of the *Sheep Shearing at Aston Clinton* allowed him to do one of the *Woburn Sheep Shearing*. This was exhibited in 1804. It is a masterpiece of meticulosity comprehending no less than eighty-eight portraits of celebrities, from the Duke of Bedford, Sir John Sinclair and Arthur Young, through practically the whole gamut of contemporary improvers in agriculture, not excluding the painter himself. Garrard's presence at Woburn must have lent a flavour to the sheep-shearing not provided by the modern photographer. Some of his models are now in private hands, but none, I believe, in any public collection.

Gordale Scar

L'Amour de Cheval

An Alderney Cow in a Barn

Though Garrard continued to add animals to the illustrations of his book and to his collection of models until 1815, Ward nowhere mentions him nor his Agricultural Museum at 28, George Street, Hanover Square. Ward doubtless thought him too small fry to be a serious competitor.

Ward would have enjoyed all the junketing amidst fine company if he was there, and would have been inspired to paint a really capital ewe for the Duke. His Grace cleared over a thousand pounds letting out on hire some seventy Southdown and New Leicester rams. This helped to pay the costs of the entertainment, though the provision of two free meals of the extravagant kind then indulged in for two hundred or more people on several successive days was no small expense.

The visit to Woburn, whether it was at the time of the sheepshearing or not, was the last journey that Ward made for the Board of Agriculture–Boydell business during 1801, but seven months of 1802 were occupied in it. He went into the wilds. According to his own mixed-up lists of the counties visited he travelled through Gloucester to Wales, Glamorgan, Caernarvon, Pembroke, Cardigan, Merioneth, Radnor, Montgomery, Monmouth, Carmarthen, Anglesey, Salop and Hereford.

Wales was a popular touring country then, and dozens of people wrote records of their journeys there. Many were appalled at the difficulties of travel, enchanted by the national costume of the women, distressed at the apparent poverty of the inhabitants of the more remote hills, and their shocking housing, especially when they had to share it for a night. All were overwhelmed by the grandeur of the mountain scenery. Extraordinarily enough Ward has left no particulars of this trip, and his correspondence is not enlightening about the conditions under which he travelled. Nor does he record any impressions, though Boydell's gig finally broke down in Anglesey, and had to be abandoned there. It realised only three and a half guineas.

Besides making studies for the livestock series Ward made almost innumerable sketches of scenes and people noticed on the way, in the villages and in the great houses, farms and cottages visited. The categorical figure of five hundred and eighty-one

D

sketches is stated by Grundy. Its precision gives it an air of truth though it may have been designed for just that purpose. An almost inconceivable industry was necessary to do all this in addition to the hundreds of animal studies that Ward made, to say nothing, as Ward complained later, of guinea dinners he was obliged to attend in London and Lewes to distribute the proposals as well as running after cattle he had heard of accidentally.

Ward was now flourishing, but he still pined for the official recognition denied him. Benjamin West, President of the Royal Academy, and Ward's friend and neighbour in Newman Street, encouraged him to believe that the time was now ripe for that much-desired event. West advised him to try something large and striking in order to wipe out the general impression that he was only an engraver. On hearing this Ward picked up the finished oil sketch of his proposed picture the *Horse and Boa Serpent*. West was so much struck by it that he there and then spoke for the finished picture when it should be completed. Ward related that it surprised everyone and that he sent it to the Academy. A few days later to his great chagrin he learned that it was rejected. It had had to be lined and repaired after an accident, having been rent from top to bottom by a piece of glass dropped by a workman who was putting in a new skylight in the studio. This picture was made for an unfortunate destiny as sometimes happens. When it was being shipped to America for exhibition in Philadelphia the ship foundered and it was lost.

Ward could hardly credit his failure to qualify as an Academician. He tried to console himself with the praise of his fellow painters, but was so disappointed that he withdrew his name as candidate for the honour he had so long coveted.

From the point of view of money and reputation this setback did not matter very much. Ward was selling his animal portraits and other pictures at such a rate that he was said to be earning as much as £50 a day, and his prices were constantly being raised as his prosperity grew. He was so far a business man. Half the nobility and gentry were on his books, and he had the support of that fine art critic and collector, Sir George Beaumont.

Sir George bought a Rubens picture, *A view of the Chateau de*

Stein Autumn, in 1803 for the then great sum of 1,500 guineas. This picture, now in the National Gallery, but not I think on show, was taken to West's studio next door to Ward's. Ward was at once called in by West to see it. He was entranced. He spent the whole day studying the picture. It was indeed universally admired by the distinguished artists called in to see it.

Ward was so greatly inspired that he shut himself up and painted his *Fighting Bulls at St. Donat's Castle*. West saw the painting and admired it; Sir George Beaumont came to see it and brought friends, 'I think,' wrote Ward, 'nine days in succession'. West brought Beckford, the author of *Vathek* and builder of a renowned folly, and told him in Ward's hearing that he considered it the perfection of execution. Presham R.A., aged and infirm, took pains to come round the table to shake hands with Ward, and tell him he had thrown down the gauntlet to Rubens and vanquished him.

This was a trifle exaggerated, but Ward had painted a magnificent picture. Every stroke is eloquent of the power behind the thick-set physique of the fighting animals, and the darkling background forms a fitting venue for a struggle between two such bovine Goliaths. When he was in Wales on Boydell's business Ward must have passed by St. Donat's Castle and probably made a sketch of the place.

Two pictures like the *Horse and Boa*, and *St. Donat's Castle*, ought to have convinced the most prejudiced of Ward's great talents as a painter. Their rejection lends some colour to Ward's impression of partiality even enmity underlying the decision. There was little comfort for him in West's sympathetic belief that the Academy did not understand Ward's powers. West said he admired Romney, who was wise enough not to attempt to exhibit his paintings in the Academy, and would have nothing to do with it. Ward should make his own private connexion; take no notice of what people said; please himself, and he would please everybody. If he painted to please others, he would please nobody. All of this was very sound.

James adopted this good advice, and held an exhibition of his work in the Newman Street studio. This rather unusual expedient was well advertised by his dispute with the Academy. Friends in the painting and fashionable world, too, made it well known in the comparatively homogenous circle of the court and the great. It was a success, and attracted still more attention to Ward's work. Morland, in the last stages of debauched degeneracy, visited it and James forgot the old time quarrel. The tender heart concealed by his tactless truculent bearing was moved to tears by his brother-in-law's terrible plight. Morland lived only a little while longer and a few days after he died James' favourite sister Anne, Morland's wife, followed her husband to the graveyard. Just after his death she declared that she had always loved him in spite of all his weaknesses and faults and could not bear to outlive him.

Ward did some more travelling during 1803, though the only record of it amongst his surviving papers is a note that a journey from Ashbourne in Derby to his home cost him £11.8.0. He does not say how long it took him, but it could not have been completed in less than several days, and the amount of his expenses is very high. He must have lived sumptuously at the best inns on his way, costly as travelling was. Compared to the then current wages of a farm worker, some 9/- or 10/- a week, it was almost extravagant.

Only two things constituted flies in James' very unctuous ointment at this time. The Boydell business was making no progress and its finances were completely unsatisfactory to him; the Royal Academy still excluded him.

He had a tremendous squabble with Boydell in 1805. The truth was that James had painted many more pictures than the firm, no longer at the peak of its success, could or was inclined to handle, and he had painted a great many scenes and events on his tours in search of livestock that were outside his contract. Here were two grand points to dispute about.

James maintained that Alderman Boydell had agreed to publish the pictures as quickly as he made them; Boydell claimed that he was entitled to issue them as and when he pleased. Since payment was made on publication his contention touched James very closely, as is easy to understand. Again Lord Somerville had scrutinised the pictures, and had reduced the number selected for issue, much to James' annoyance and financial loss.

James presented Boydells with an account in 1805 coupled with a fierce diatribe upon their methods, and a stern demand for more money. It is not an account that is very easy to understand, but he claimed to have produced a hundred and fifty pictures besides those painted and sent home. He demanded a payment of twenty pounds a week for the time spent in travelling and expenses at one guinea a day. Not unnaturally he wanted to be reimbursed for the many repairs to the gig. Boydell, whose business at the Shakespeare Gallery was steadily declining, firmly refused these demands, declaring that he had already paid more than the agreed value of the pictures sent in. There was something else that James failed to take into account. When he was away on these journeys Mrs. Ward had been in the habit of applying to Boydell for money in advance to meet her by no means inconsiderable housekeeping expenses, including provision for the footman in a silver-trimmed livery, and all that accompanied that style of living.

The end of the Boydell business is hidden in the same fog as so much of James' other affairs. Many more letters were exchanged between the parties, but no perceptible conclusion was reached, unless it was the sad one James recorded for the *Art Journal* of 1860 in the last year of his life. He had visited a great portion of the United Kingdom, and painted more than two hundred portraits of animals, but the King, the patrons and the publishers died, the society (i.e. the Board of Agriculture) sank, leaving him a loser by many hundred pounds. These miserable events did not take place at once as his note would suggest; but successively during the next two decades. Whether this job just petered out or whether James ceased to do anything further is not clear. It ended in disappointment, annoyance and trouble and died from these causes. One thing it most certainly did. It established James as the leading horse and cattle painter of the day, and his work in the genre has been appreciated by people of taste ever since.

It was during this year when the Boydell business began

dying of inanition that James, encouraged perhaps by his friends, made another attack on the Jericho walls of the Royal Academy.

Ward had on hand some pictures painted during the Welsh tour for Sir Watkyns Wynne, and another *Sheepwashing*. These were hung in the Academy exhibition, but their painter was not elected. Next year he tried again, but a quarrel with the hanging committee about the disposition of the pictures on the walls forced Ward, or so he argued, to take them home again. He used them as the basis of another exhibition of his work at Newman Street. This exhibition aroused nearly as much interest as the earlier one. For a brief space Ward became the fashion. He was independent of academic distinction. He had achieved his ambition without it, and when, after his galaxy of paintings, embracing one of his *Pigs*, and another in the tradition of the old masters, *The Infant Christ embracing the Cross*, had been shown the following year, he was reluctantly made an Associate. A few years later he became an R.A.

The religious subject exhibited was a demonstration of James Ward's determination to break away from the curse, as he felt it, of being only an animal painter. It was a determination strengthened by the opposition of his fellows, and solidified as he progressed through life, causing him to follow a path full of thorns and pitfalls for one of his peculiar talents. Blessed as he was with a photographic eye for the lines of animals and for the beauty of the natural scenes in which they lived, and with a taste similar to Morland's, fiercely as he would have denied it, for rustic persons and country buildings, Ward was seduced from his proper work into attempts to reproduce and outdo the great allegorical pictures of the past. It is unfortunate that it is almost impossible for anyone so vain and self-centred as Ward to recognise his limitations or even the sphere in which he could and did shine.

Deep religiosity, that later became fanaticism, almost hallucination, was already beginning to darken Ward's mind, where in the shadows his old grievances against the world continued to flourish like fungi in a dark damp cellar. Newton, his favourite preacher, died in 1807, and a little later he fell under the malign influence of Irving, that witting or unwitting charlatan, who

spoke in jargon that he and his deluded followers believed to be
an unknown language. His influence on Ward was fell. James'
mind was already darkened by the shadows of a gloomy faith
restricted by its narrow prohibitions and poisoned by the de-
lusions and infantile hatreds derived from the shocking conditions
of his childhood. Irving's influence made him even more combative, and filled him with envy, jealousy and malice towards all
who dared to trespass upon the boundaries of his own chosen, but
despised, trade of animal painter.

Fifty years later these feelings still polluted his aged dreams
of the past. He scarified Herring in one of his lengthy letters to
his devoted son George. 'If I had painted nothing but Horses,
Why the Jockeys and Jockey Gents would prefer the works of
Herring and a specimen is now sent to me as one of his crack
efforts.' This was of three horses' heads 'villainously drawn, feeding on a scanty meal of wiry hay and one of them nibbling at vine
leaves'. The rest of this letter is lost. This is gross severity towards
a man who was not born till 1795 when James was already on a
rising tide of prosperity. On this tide he was still being carried
when Herring went to Doncaster in 1814. There he tried to paint
the Duke of Hamilton's horse, William, the winner of the St.
Leger. The attempt was a failure though chance took a hand
and made him into a famous painter of racehorses. Ward was
stupid to be jealous of a man of a later generation, one of his
successors, though right enough to be critical of bad work. He was
in no way absurd to be watchful of the success of his contemporaries. Jealousy is a mental attitude that can easily become an
obsession, and most human beings have to guard against it.
James was incapable of doing this. He made the fiercest attacks
upon his brother-in-law Chalon, who was a successful animal
painter, but whose life was not very commendable. James could
find no words harsh enough to condemn him. He emphasised
Chalon's drunkenness and immorality, common enough faults of
that day, when Lord Chesterfield consulted Ward about employing
Chalon at his country residence. He did his best to prevent
Chalon becoming an Associate of the Royal Academy for reasons
other than his ability to paint, and he tried to influence the tone

of the obituary written by Hall, in the *Art Journal* after Chalon died.

James' jealousy and contempt for his competitors was a measure of his own success and recognition. This child of the slums was now a friend of the great and noble, and his popularity so great that his charges began to outrun discretion. These led to disputes with his clients. Many of them were enormously wealthy, but like all wealthy people these landowners and leaders of farming were unwilling to be overcharged, or to have the agreed prices of paintings increased. Another thing that they must have hated was the unmeasured language in which Ward couched his demands.

Lord Darnley, who had commissioned a portrait of a little dog, thought fifty guineas enough for this picture. James apparently did not. In the course of an acid controversy his lordship pointed out that Sir Joshua Reynolds had added a little dog to a picture of a young lady when requested to do so. He made no extra charge for it. Lord Darnley's letter added that no one else would have charged so much. Ward modestly replied that in comparison with himself, Rubens was gross and vulgar. This was no more than the over-whelming vanity of an ego that always failed to make a just comparison of its own merits with those of others. By his innate constitution this would have been an impossible task for a man like Ward.

Disagreements now became continual in James' career, though there was sometimes the shadow of justification for them. Occasionally there was some competition for a completed picture, leading to higher bids than the charge agreed upon with the person who had ordered it. Sir Thomas Lawrence tried to over-bid for a picture that had been painted for a Mr. Barnes, a London stockbroker, but here the strict ruling of his uneasy conscience supported James in selling it to Barnes at the lower price. What is to be made of such a man?

All this queasiness of temperament failed to undermine James' position though it might well have done so. His output was large, but his work did not confine him to London. He was continually travelling to distant parts of the country to see clients or for un-

stated reasons. When the whole country was on the alert under
the threat of invasion by the large army and flotilla of flat-
bottomed boats Napoleon had assembled at Boulogne, James went
to Alnwick on the invitation of the Duke of Northumberland.
He was not concerned with the crisis in the military affairs of the
nation, and paid no more attention to it than did Coke of Norfolk.
Both were too absorbed in their own occupations.

The only impact that national affairs made upon James' sensi-
bilities was a review of his private forces carried out by the Duke.
James was an interested spectator, possibly attracted by the
pictorial value of the scene. Some fifteen hundred horsemen and
unnumbered foot were ranged in the Castle yard, and the Duke
made them all an impassioned speech. James made no comment
upon the speech in his scanty record of the occasion.

The date of this visit is not very clear, but James had been in
Wales again in 1807. By inference he suggests that it was in 1811
and it may well have been, but it was probably before then. If
it was, James did an almost impossible amount of travelling in
that year. Some of his odd notes headed *Tour to the North* pur-
port to relate to this journey, but if so it was a Chestertonian
roundabout tour like going to Birmingham by way of Beachy
Head.

He left London on the 27th of June for Poole in Dorset. He
passed through Southampton and comments that Ringwood was
beautiful and so was the New Forest. He visited Brownsea
Island by the courtesy of Mr. Allen, Comptroller of the Customs,
who carried him there in the revenue cutter. He saw the ruins
of Corfe Castle and Swanage, then a village of some 2,000 people.
Salisbury spire was higher, but not so elegant as Lichfield; Old
Sarum a tiny village with a windmill. He went to Wilton
through Bemerton where the Rev. George Herbert had lived
and written. A primitive waterworks had been made at one or
other of these villages by carrying a stream of water through the
houses. Malmesbury had a very remote ruin. Cirencester was a
clean neat town, all whitewashed. Malvern hills were bold and
fine. He slept at Tewkesbury. He visited Tabley Park which he
left on the 27th of July. Manchester was large and bleak and

Londonified. Blackburn was all black. Whalley Abbey fine, and there is a note here that Lord Portsmouth was fond of driving his own dung carts and ringing church bells, a queer mixture of tastes. On the 6th of August Ward was at Gisburne where he was to paint a life-sized picture of a roan. He left Gisburne on the 30th of August and visited Tabley Park again, and then went through Stone and Holme Chapel, Newcastle and on to Wades Bridge. In another place Ward comments on Sir Joshua Reynolds' altar piece in glass at Lichfield which had some fine effects of beauty rather than grandeur, the head wanting in dignity and character. Here he saw the 4th Irish Dragoons Guards going through on their way to embark for Spain. They were very fine men, but Ward wished they had been better employed.

Not satisfied with this exhausting trek all round the country not an excessive journey for a summer motor tour, but which James had to do by horse transport over vile roads, he set out on a walk through the Lowlands of Scotland in the autumn of the year. Grundy suggests that this pedestrian expedition was undertaken for pleasure. If so the anticipation of enjoyment remained sadly unfulfilled.

Readers of Smollett's *Roderick Random*, Scott's *Rob Roy*, and Stevenson's *Kidnapped*, will be well acquainted with the hardships Ward encountered. His experiences were little better, if no worse, than those of the heroes of these romances.

Ward made a few comments upon the conditions of the English part of the journey, but what he found in Scotland filled him with dismay, experienced traveller though he was. He possessed his share of hardihood and endurance; it was put to the most severe test on this pleasure jaunt. Of course he had the seeing eye and could not but use it. Everywhere he went he was on the lookout for fine scenes, splendid animals and odd and entertaining persons, things and places that he might record by pencil, brush or style.

The walking tour in Scotland was so unpleasant that his mind must have been almost exclusively occupied with his immediate physical needs. The prosperous painter, friend of the great and wealthy and guest in country mansions, was not prepared for the poor meals served in Scottish village inns despite his experiences all over England and in the wildest parts of Wales. Kale brose has been greatly praised, and was then being strongly recommended to the poverty-stricken farm labourers of the south as a more economical dish than the white bread to which they were accustomed. They preferred their dole in bread and nearly all of them had to have this dole under the conditions of astronomically high prices and infinitesimally low wages then ruling. This was recognised by the general adoption of a system of making up the inadequate wages to a subsistence level by a payment from the rates to a fixed standard, a specified number of loaves of bread for each member of the family, husband, wife and children. The sternest exhortation failed to convince these misguided people that they ought to eat kale brose. Their reasons were just the opposite to those of James Ward who liked it no more than they. It was the usual fare and the only thing to be had in some of the tiny inns of the Lowlands. The diners dipped it from a common bowl with a wooden spoon. When the food was more luxurious as at Lanark it was no great shakes. Two courses of dirty salt dry fish, soup made of rice and cabbage and a 'stinking knuckle bone of ham' completed it. Discomfort may have lent emphasis to Ward's sense of epithet. Bad eggs, butter prepared with no care for cleanliness, full of cow hairs and as stiff as mortar, coal dust in the gravy making the meat uneatable, formed further grounds of well deserved complaint. This miserable diet was occasionally sanctified by the service of a freshly caught trout.

These meals did nothing to mitigate the poor accommodation though it can have been no worse than Ward had encountered in Wales. Some of the inns were of only one room, a kitchen-dining-living room and dormitory as well. Here, to Ward's great perturbation, the poorer guests disrobed and went to bed naked and unashamed. Where a room was to be had it was often one that opened out into others, as is so frequent in older buildings and cottages. A sleeper might be disturbed by some other guest going to bed, provided he could sleep at all in the dirty, damp sheets so often supplied, and undisturbed by his unwanted and tormenting bedfellows.

The weather was bad and what with catching cold, getting
blistered feet, and suffering from gravel, a disease not caused by
the walking tour, James had a miserable time of it. His indomitable spirit drove him on, and he made many sketches and
walked innumerable miles living largely upon milk and whiskey.
The author had a very similar experience during the blizzard of
March, 1916, now a forgotten event.

This was not James' first visit to the Lowlands; but it was very
different from his previous experience. Then he was the travelling companion of Lord Somerville and his guest at Melrose.
Both had been overnight guests of Sir Walter Scott at Abbotsford,
which was only reached after some difficulty and danger because
the Tweed was in spate. Like so many other people visiting great
writers after being impressed by their work Ward was a little
disappointed with Scott at first; his opinion changed late in the
evening. Scott's appearance and simplicity did not, to Ward's
mind, run on all fours with the impression James had received
from Scott's romantic works; but when he recited a poem he had
received from Mr. Campbell 'his countenance lighted, his eyes
sparkled and his nostrils opened like those of a blood horse at a
race course'. This was the real Walter Scott. Somerville had
commissioned four large landscapes that Ward painted during
this visit.

The contrast of the two journeys was very great, and James
must have been sensibly affected by it, but hard as it was the
second tour provided new subjects to sketch and reflect upon. At
the seats of the mighty where he was more frequently entertained when on painting commissions, James was welcome both
as an artist and as a man. He possessed the qualifications most in
esteem amongst the country gentlemen. He was a dead shot and
an accomplished horseman who could often vanquish them at
their own favourite field sports. His exaggerated independence
of character, often the accompaniment of genius and more often
that of persons of James' early experience, kept him respected in
this severely manly society. He did not fail in punctilio toward
those of higher rank than himself, but he demanded that they did
not fail in punctilio towards him in return. A tale is told that he

corrected the Marquis of Londonderry for addressing a letter to him as 'Mr.' when he was entitled to be addressed as 'Esquire', a point that his lordship must have appreciated, if only because it was the sort of thing that he had been taught to consider and to give weight to. There is nothing so successful as snobbery in a snobbish society, provided that it is well grounded, though James was not cold and calculating enough to take that into proper account. His impetuous self-consideration did as much for him.

At about this time a strikingly characteristic incident occurred. James was at Bradby doing some work for the Earl of Chesterfield, and his stay was prolonged enough for his daughter to be invited to accompany him. She resembled her famous mother, one-time toast at Almacks, and her beauty and charm greatly attracted the Earl's nephew, Lieut. Stanhope. These young people found each other pleasing, and James began to entertain hopes that a marriage might result, a denouement that would have gratified him exceedingly. Unfortunately he tried to rush matters by going to the Earl about it. The Earl, head of a family of noble rank, would not countenance such a match. James, in high dudgeon, took his daughter back to town and the affair collapsed, to his chagrin.

James' family then consisted of four boys and two girls, a great drain on a father's resources. Henry, the eldest, was weak minded; Matilda, too, indulged in fits of hysteria and was of the type that shines upon a social occasion, but is difficult in the home; James Claude, who had some parts, was erratic and led an unfortunate life; George Raphael was a solid citizen who spent most of his life at his father's behest rather than at his own choice; Emma was religious and followed her father in the purity of her moral character; Somerville the youngest died in childhood.

What exactly happened to the Boydell work is not clear. James had made a great many pictures and a good many were engraved. At least sixty are definitely catalogued and include horses, cattle, sheep and pigs of breeds scattered widely throughout the country. The balance of the work is likely to have been used for other purposes though Somerville had 'laid aside' a good many of the drawings James made.

He had plenty of work without it, and plenty of patrons in spite of his ill temper and remarkable bearing. One of these was the son and heir of Lord Ribblesdale. He had been fascinated by the *Boa* painting when he saw it in the Newman Street studio. On his father's Yorkshire estate was Gordale Scar, that remarkable natural phenomenon. It was a wild piece of scenery. The Scar was so tremendous that artists despaired of it, while they were enthralled by it. No one thought it a possible subject. On the contrary everyone, including the great connoisseur Sir George Beaumont, declared that it could not be painted. This was just the sort of challenge that awakened all of James' enthusiasm and his morbid desire to attempt the impossible.

The opportunity came when Lord Ribblesdale planned to extend his dining room, and wanted a large picture to embellish one of the end walls. James was invited to Yorkshire and asked to paint the scene. This he undertook with alacrity, and, despite the terrifying difficulties, he produced a work of great genius. The sombre hues of the cliff face, the shadows in the gorge, the awe that the scene inspired were all collected by the very real fact that Ward's soul reflected the shadows and overwhelming impression of the littleness of humanity before such an inert and soulless mass. The huge strength of the white bull in the foreground, characteristic of nearly all Ward's bulls, is again a reflection of his own physique – bull-necked as it was – though at the same time true to the nature of the beast whose colour lends a welcome ray of light to the composition.

The picture, completed in 1812, was and is a triumph and is now, it is understood, housed in the cellars of the Tate Gallery; but like all Ward's triumphs it led to a bitter disappointment. Lord Ribblesdale proclaimed it too great a work of art to be buried in a remote country house in Yorkshire, possibly a tactful excuse for not wanting to keep it himself. He sent it to the British Museum, for the proposed National Gallery. After that it was nobody's baby for half a century. Years later, when he had moved out of London to Roundcroft at Cheshunt, Ward wrote an undated letter to his lordship saying that it was only two hours' ride from London and asking him to visit him there. 'Nothing in the distance from London is more pleasant,' wrote James, 'than the road through Hornsey and the green lanes all the way to my cottage. After Hornsey you pass through Enfield to Cheshunt Church one mile beyond which is a lane leading to Newgate Street and opposite Mrs. Russell's lodge at Cheshunt Park.' James added that he often drove to London in one and a half hours.

There is nothing in Ward's papers to show whether Lord Ribblesdale accepted the invitation, but much later, judging from the handwriting, James wrote to an unknown person disputing that the picture was the property of the representative of his lordship, a claim that the authorities of the British Museum believed to be valid. These authorities then said that they had returned the picture to Lord Ribblesdale, but in 1857 someone at the Museum wrote to Ward to contradict a statement that the picture was housed by them in a damp cellar. The letter stated that Lord Ribblesdale gave the picture in 1830, but resumed his gift in that year, and this may have been when Ward asked him to come to Roundcroft. Finally, after all these misfortunes, the picture was bought by the trustees of the National Gallery for £1,200 from the heirs of Lord Ribblesdale, and now occupies a pseudo-honoured place in the national collection. All this would have been more than galling to anyone and more especially to a man like Ward, who believed that every man's hand was against him, a feeling that the misadventures of this painting through so many years did nothing to alleviate.

Ward must have seen the hand of God in all his tribulations, believing as he did in the fury of hell fire for the punishment of sinners. His misfortunes must have been for the chastening of his spirit. After Newton's death when he became a follower of Irving, his religion became even more sombre. Irving was a near neighbour. He converted the Galleries, built by West and Bacon in the gardens at the back of their Newman Street houses, into a pulpit. From it he spake in an unknown tongue.

The mystery of this gibberish, consciously or unconsciously adopted by Irving, was something to intrigue the public in that superstitious age, greedy of marvels as all such times are, and

indeed as everybody had for long been. Popular credulity knew
no bounds. The rich consulted astrologers, the poor had recourse
to wise men and cunning women. Nothing was too absurd to be
credited. Any curious spectacle was attributed to supernatural
causes by the ignorant and all flocked to see it, anxious to believe,
and to be duped by knaves.

As Southey scornfully said, 'Everything that is strange or that
is called strange, a tall man or a short man, a Gostre or an
Albino, a white negro or a spotted negro, which may be made at
any time with little difficulty and no pain, a great ox or a fat pig,
no matter what the wonder be and no matter how monstrous and
disgusting, it will attract crowds in England. Posture masters and
stone eaters have demonstrated strange and anomalous powers in
the human body, and the docility of animals has been practised
upon for the sake of immediate gain.'

Comets and meteors, now recognised as harmless natural
phenomena, were feared with an overwhelming dread. The
brilliant comet that shone in the heavens during the summer of
1811 almost caused a national panic. It portended worse wars
and disasters than those already afflicting tormented Europe. The
world was about to perish in an awful cataclysm of fire and the
dread prophecies of Mother Shipton about to be fulfilled before
their due date. The Apocalypse and the Books of Daniel and
Revelation were ransacked for texts to prove that the comet foretold the end of the age. 'Day after day as the expiring light
brought the comet more clearly into view, the fears of the
ploughman and the reaper increased in a tenfold degree. Night
after night in the course of that long, dry summer vast crowds
employed the hours, usually devoted by the world to sleep, in
walking through the fields and open spaces, or in sitting at the
open windows in order to gaze upon the matchless glories of this
brilliant comet.' James Hogg, the Ettrick shepherd, then at the
height of his fame, wrote some verses about it, but few paid any
attention to the reassuring words of contemporary scientists.

Rarely could anyone be found among the ten million total
population, who was immune to the pretences of the swindlers
and imposters who practised upon the boundless credulity of the

majority. Tales of mystery, superstition and horror like the
gothic romances of Anne Radcliffe, M. G. Lewis and Mrs.
Edgeworth, were the popular literature of the educated. The
ignorant fully believed in stories of similar terrors, told again
and again round their own firesides in the dark winter evenings,
when the flickering light added to their delightful tremors, or
over a pot of beer in the murky semi-darkness of the village
alehouse. Scarcely a young person but had a firm belief in
spirits, not an old man who had not seen or heard some supernatural manifestation.

'The fays' it was believed still led their mazy dance over the
green rings by the light of the pale moon on the Sussex Downs,
and in the forest glades of Hampshire. Brownies and pixies still
rejoiced to hear the solemn tones of the curfew bell that they
might begin their gambols under the rowan tree, their favourite
trysting place, and lead benighted travellers astray on the bogs of
Dartmoor. Drowned men still hailed their own names in stormy
weather near the spot where they had perished, off the Lincolnshire seaboard. A mysterious vessel, tall, square-rigged with black
sails beating up against wind and tide, was sometimes seen in the
Channel and betokened death to all who caught a glimpse of it.

The colour of Ward's mind was only too easily tinged with all
these fantasia. To a more ordinary degree it was open and recep-
tive to miracles, wonders and mysteries, its whole trend having
been turned in this direction from his earliest years. His continual excursions into the more remote and isolated parts of the
country had added quite exceptional opportunities of hearing
stories of ghosts, witches, warlocks and wonders. Where the
ordinary man could only mystify and terrify himself in that age
of almost static population by repeating old and time-worn, but
none the less believed, stories of dread and wonder, Ward could
collect them on a national scale.

When he was touring in Wales on the Boydell business in 1802
he stayed with Sir Robert Vaughan in Merioneth and learned
from him a wonderful story of a woman who had lived without
food for the better part of a century. Ward's curiosity was at once
inflamed, and off he went to see this marvel. He was allowed to

see her in bed at her cottage at Tanyralt near Dolgelly on the opposite bank of the river from Barmouth. Her name was Mary Thomas. She was then seventy-seven, a sufficiently magical age. Ward accepted the tale he was told that this Mary Thomas did not eat, did not evacuate her bowels or bladder, and that if she ate her stomach threw it off in a bout of sickness. She was purged by suffering, and had a marked character of serenity. Pity and resignation appeared to Ward the prominent features of her character. Ward was again in Wales in 1807, and Mary Thomas was still in the same state though his memory of the place was not too good and he had some difficulty in finding her. When he did he drew a portrait of her and made other pictures. On this occasion one Robert Edwards was his guide and interpreter. By profession Edwards was a guide to Cader Idris, and the mere existence of such a job demonstrated the growth of tourism at the end of the eighteenth century. Ward found him a picturesque figure, and drew him riding on his mule. This time, too, Ward found a brother of this extraordinary woman. He was seventy-two, and claimed to be the youngest of six brothers and sisters. His sister Mary had, he told Ward, suffered from an illness like smallpox when she was thirteen, and this had started her peculiar condition. The woman had already achieved a place in literature before Ward discovered her. Thomas Pennant saw her in 1770 when he made his *Journey to Snowdon* and was then told that the first illness took place when Mary was seven. It attacked her again at twenty-seven when she remained insensible for two and a half days.

James Ward, like Thomas Pennant, accepted this remarkable story as gospel until he went to visit a woman at Tutbury who was in a similar state, though her famine had lasted the comparatively short space of six or seven years. This woman, Anne Moore, was introduced to Ward by Jackson of Tutbury in 1809. Her affliction began after she had attended a man named Samuel Orange who was suffering from an offensive but unspecified disease. He died on 30 October, 1806, and as a result of her ministrations Anne had to give up work and to take to her bed; she could eat nothing and subsisted on drinking a little tea

without milk. An odd feature of her malady was that food brought
on an offensive smell of orange, a quite miraculous result from
nursing a man named Orange. Anne kept her window open day
and night, which everyone at that time thought dangerous,
especially at night. She always sat upright in bed. She took snuff.
This was altogether too much even for the monstrous credulity
of those days. Anne Moore's neighbours believed her an impostor,
and her children and relatives were always insulted when they
appeared in the streets.

The woman's condition was tested by a sceptical Dr. Hender-
son. He kept her under observation in another house for sixteen
days, but Ward was at first disinclined to believe the fraud
exposed by the honourable doctor. A further observation was
arranged, but food was smuggled in by a daughter after she had
driven the observers out of the house under a pretence of extreme illness. In his account of these events which he published
as *Some accounts of Mary Thomas of Tanyralt in Merioneth-
shire . . . and Ann Moore . . . accompanied with portraits and
illustrated etchings by James Ward R.A.* at his own expense in
1813, Ward somewhat naïvely remarks that the exposure of
Anne Moore cast some doubts on Mary Thomas. He regretted
that it was not possible to test Mary's claims as she had died in the
interim. The illustrations to the book are fine and afford an
insight into the furnishings and general appearance of a Welsh
cottage and the appearance of the Welsh peasantry. *

The exposure of Anne Moore did not prevent Ward from re-
cording other impressions of the marvellous. Southey's remark
about dwarfs is confirmed by the interest Ward, none so large
a man himself, took in the guard of a coach on which he travelled
to Lea Castle in the summer of 1814. The guard looked like a
little fat chubby boy about seven or eight years old. He was only
three feet ten inches tall, if such a measurement is tall, but was
very talkative and interesting, so much so that Ward got out and
rode in the dicky with him. James, clever with his fingers, made
him a loop to hang his horn in; it was very nearly as long as

* The only copy of this book known to me is in the Library of the
Royal Academy by whose courtesy I have been able to examine it.

himself, 'but he blew it famously'. He was full of pranks, and
when he wanted a bit of fun he made himself more ludicrous
than he was by wearing a great wig and a hat as big as an
umbrella. He was a happy little man, and sang all day as they
drove along, taking his ditties from a book he carried. It had
seen so much use it was almost worn out. This homunculus was
born in 1788, was married, and had one child.

With all this superstition about, the phenomenon of insanity
was naturally looked upon with horror as demoniac possession, or
an unbalanced mind was so incredibly humorous as to be comic.
Bedlam was indeed a fashionable rendezvous on visiting days
when crowds went to jeer at or gaze upon the unfortunates con-
fined there in chains and often in semi-nudity. One of Ward's
friends, a Dr. Woodey, kept a private madhouse at Tamworth,
and in 1815 Ward journeyed down from London to visit him.
Here he saw another wonder. The enormous strength of a person
in an ecstasy of insanity is, and I suppose was, a matter of common talk and general belief. Ward was shown a man working in
the garden who had made some progress towards recovery.
Rather unflatteringly he compared this man's appearance with
that of Northcote R.A., which doubtless endeared him to that
man if he ever learned of it.

When he was ill the convalescent pulled down the curtain
rods of his bedstead with his hands alone, and twisted them into
what he called a true lover's knot. It was so firmly made that it
required a blacksmith with his fire and tools to untwist it. 'Is
not this like what we read in the Gospel of a man possessed with
a legion of Devils that no Chains and cord could bind?' asked
Ward. Thirty-five years later he was contemptuous of a *Church
of Christ* which had exploded the idea or turned it into a jest.
'Now in the March of Intellect' of 1850.

Ward may have visited Woodey's madhouse in this year. He
was at Bradby when the awkward circumstances of his daughter's
almost-love-affair cropped up. A letter of this year to Lord Stanhope suggests this. It is a lengthy and complex exegesis on prices
and methods of payment. Ward declared that it was usual for an
artist to get half his fee after the first sitting of a commission. His

prices were, he wrote, plainly set up in his gallery. A full-length portrait, life size, was 250 guineas, a second figure 125 guineas extra, so Lord Stanhope's picture was 357 guineas; the ladies 500 guineas; three common half lengths 120 guineas; the drawings of the bucks 25 guineas each. A not unprofitable visit; although Ward graciously added, 'The drawings of the Tree with those of the children do me the honour to accept.'

Lord Grenville, writing from Dropmore, accepted a picture of his greyhounds with which he was very delighted. He enquired what he owed with an equanimity that might have surprised Ward if he had not been so assured of his own value despite frequent squabbles with his patrons on that very subject.

He could hardly have been less than flattered by an eulogistic letter from Dr. Woodey recommending one Webb to him. Webb was apparently an aspiring painter or engraver, and, according to Woodey, was a poor, industrious, anxious man who had besides a wife and six children. He intended to visit all the exhibitions and to see all the single pictures he could during his stay in London. Ward was asked whether he could get him permission to see the Marquis of Stafford's collection. What happened does not emerge.

Ward may have been in Wiltshire during this year to recruit. His spirit, health and energy were renewed, but in his anxiety to accept all the work offered because he was always in need of money, he got himself into difficulties by promising more than he could possibly perform. To this time may belong such water colours as *A Wiltshire Hind* and possibly *Rustic with bucket*, both reproduced by Grundy.

Victory at Waterloo put a final period to the French Wars in 1815, that year when Ward was so very busy. This victory, which he had hardly noticed at the time, and which was belittled by a young officer he met on the way to Tamworth, was to play a major part in James' later life. The young officer had a great hatred of Wellington, and thought little of the battle that was in very truth won, not only by steadfast troops of whom Wellington himself had no very great opinion, but also very materially by the luck of the England to which we, her sons, are still so devoted.

This year of great triumph for the nation was the year which saw the beginning of the end for Ward. It was at the zenith of his fame and triumph too. His extravagance and egotism knew no bounds. He was filled with an illusion of grandeur, a feeling that was fed by the praise and adulation of his clients.

The writing of his book on the two fasting women had convinced Ward that he had other talents besides those of painting and engraving, and he occupied much of his spare time in the composition of verse that sank to the very nadir of futility. He did not think so; he thought no less highly of these jejune, puerile efforts, than he did of his very real success in his proper medium of expression. Looking back from 1851 he wrote to his son George, sending him a poem that a misguided clergyman, the Rev. Mr. Foster, had told him was like *L'Allegro*. If only, he lamented, he had had Milton's education he would have been as great a poet as Milton himself, a piece of egotism that can rarely have been equalled and rarely imitated. His own birthplace had been somewhere near where Milton was born, a somewhat fantastic claim, which even if true, is unlikely to have had any influence upon the relative genius of the two men.

When Ozeas Humphrey brought Earl Fitzwilliam to Newman Street the Earl had told Ward that St. Donat's Castle had been painted by a giant. 'Those were the days when I was the fashion ... When I was at Almacks with the Duke of Northumberland he told me I had unfortunately too much talent ... What I might have been with the education of Rubens, and have lived at a period when allegory and sumptuous history was relished, but now we must go back to the infancy of art ... Alas! Alas! what is fashion but what I have described in my *Defence of the Beard*.'

With all his great income, his unceasing industry, and the almost uniform excellence of his vast output, James' expenses outran the constable. His financial extravagance, almost stupidity as such behaviour always seems, led him from the path of success to follow one that led in exactly the opposite direction.

He was an enamoured apostle of Edward Irving, as already said, and no less misguided than he. Irving, fanciful, even deluded as he was, possessed a sweetness of character that James entirely lacked, though Irving was roundly condemned in the powerful language of the day by his opponents. The Rev. John Hawker called Irving a son of Belial and in the name of the everlasting Jehovah proclaimed him the 'Balaam' of the present-day 'Gentile generation of vipers', the false prophet of a people 'who hold the truth in unrighteousness'.

The effect of Ward's absorption in Irving's teachings was deplorable. The side of his character that his early life had forced into prominence became more marked. He held himself aloof as one of God's gifted, a man of unmeasurable talents, one who must not be criticised, one who was capable of all achievement, certainly not a man whose sole claim to fame was an ability to make photographic pictures of people and animals, of small domestic affairs, of trivial country scenes.

At this period the balance of his mind was disturbed. He dreamed dreams and saw visions, and he was himself convinced that he soon would demonstrate to the world the might of his capacity in some vast and extraordinary work.

Maybe he could have continued to be held in respect for his very real talents had he been a different man, but one of the most pronounced of all his talents was his contempt for the achievement of other men. He had not the tact to refrain from expressing it, a most sure and certain way of making enemies who would one day rise up to destroy him, if he did not succeed in destroying himself. He failed to realise that his own character was imperfect; he never knew he was a man amongst other men, subject to the same weaknesses, many rather more pronounced in himself than in others. No, the only frailty he recognised was their inability to accept him at his own valuation. This fundamental defect of character rapidly brought him down from the high place to which his talents had raised him, though he continued to paint successfully and to exhibit each year in the salons of the Royal Academy for another forty years.

CHAPTER VI

The Waterloo Allegory fiasco and Retreat to Roundcroft

Most people now living know very well the relief of victory and peace after years of war. Modern men can easily understand and sympathise with the spontaneous outburst of joy that followed Waterloo, the victorious climax of wars that had lasted more than twenty years. A feeling of security followed. Our ancestors felt certain of their own powers to win the peace as well, and the peace must be celebrated. The British Institution consequently decided to celebrate Waterloo in a suitable and permanent manner. They would commission a great painting to commemorate the victory that filled the country so full of pride.

The idea was that a large allegorical picture should be painted and hung in Chelsea Hospital, then being rebuilt under the guidance of the great contemporary architect, Sir John Soane. The job was put up to competition and sketches of the proposed design were required to be submitted. Ward thought the competition a great opportunity to demonstrate his ability in the allegorical and heroical line in which he had always hoped to shine. Though the leading artists of the day sent in designs, Ward's was much the most elaborate. It was accordingly selected. Possibly for that very reason, something that must have appealed strongly to the judges, who were men of their time.

Allegory was not, in fact, one of the inspirations of that age, and taste for that sort of picture was consequently not developed. The Gothic and picturesque builders mistook complexity for beauty. Ward's design was so complicated and the allegory so involved that it could only be understood with the help of a

written explanation. This was the merit, subtlety of idea and
abounding but not very helpful suggestion, that made him the
choice of the Institution. A thousand guineas was the financial
reward, and undying fame the expected spiritual meed.

Ward could not let well alone. His temperament was against
any such simple behaviour. When the idea for a commemorative
undertaking was first mooted, he produced a grandoise scheme
of his own. This was no less than Three Temples of Art, one for
each kingdom. They were to include all the visual arts in great
galleries. Sections were to be devoted to literature, science and
industry to the greater glory of Britain. Each country would then
have a University of the Visual Arts and a National Gallery of
Painting and Sculpture as well as a Museum of Science and
Industry. The idea is a fine example of the vastness of Ward's
conceptions, and of the degree of their practicality. They have
some of the character of H. G. Wells' later exordiums on what
the future of civilisation would be like. In some sense his ideas
have since been carried out, but not as a celebration of the
victory of Waterloo. He was not so insane as he has been described, though there is no question but that he was unable to
conceive of any limit to his powers. When all is said and done
few men are effective judges of their own abilities.

Ward's proposals were set forth in a long memorandum and
supported by a lengthy exegesis of a religious nature justifying
the triune character of his suggestions by comparison with the
triune foundations of the true religion. The tortuous and involved argument depending, as such arguments so often do,
upon analogy drawn between completely incongruous objects, is
almost incomprehensible. It reads like ecstasy, some subliminal
possession similar to that from which Blake suffered, and which
led to his admired, strange paintings, his lovely short poems, and
his thaumaturgical long poems.

Blake's mind suffered from the odd religion he followed, so did
James Ward's. The oddities of his religion, grafted upon his early
puritanical, extremist piety, led him still further astray from his
proper task, a task well within his capacity, and moreover to the
taste of the time. He could have been satisfied to be animal painter

in ordinary to the agricultural nobility and gentry in addition to being a famous painter of rural scenes and rural life; but this was not enough for him. He had to depict on canvas the feverish imaginings of a mind that was sick, if not acutely disordered, by his lofty conception of himself and the fantastic inspirations derived from worship in Irving's chapel, where the pastor and the congregation, fired with the spirit, declaimed in an unknown tongue, language that conveyed nothing but frenzy. Ward was not free from these ebullitions, but they overflowed from his own egotism. Always his own greatness, the large message he must deliver through his art, or verbally, was the subject of his prophecy.

The *Allegory* was a misguided undertaking; it failed. Had it succeeded Ward would not be the half-forgotten painter he is, but does not deserve to be, today. The reason is obvious. Neither Ward nor the time was the occasion for such a production. Allegory as a medium for the diffusion of morality was dead, and other means were necessary to promote it. Neither Ward nor his contemporaries could recognise this. Consequently the whole project was doomed before it was commenced.

Almost immediately he received the commission Ward demanded that he should be allowed to increase the size of the proposed picture. The first plan was for a painting 14' by 12', but Ward found that his complex conception would be cramped on this relatively small scale. It was accordingly agreed that the canvas should be 20' by 14'; but even this would not allow of life-size figures, so the size was finally made 35' by 21'. This monstrous canvas had to be woven for the job, and there was no space big enough for it in Ward's studio. He had it fixed on rollers and suspended from the roof so that he could open the space on which he was working. This must have added enormously to the difficulties of the task, but Ward refused to be defeated.

James cast aside most of his other work, and his income went down with a bang. He would only accept work that he could do in London in order to keep the pot boiling, though he did travel occasionally. He would only do other work in intervals snatched

from the production that was to be the keystone of his fame, and
make him the acknowledged leader of the art in England. He
went at the work with that unflagging determination, so marked
a facet of his character. He spent hours and days in the British
Museum studying the Elgin marbles; he sought inspiration in
additional devotion, praying to be endowed with light from the
spirit of his awful God.

The result was appalling. The picture, which was not finished
until 1822, was fantastic in conception; its meaning was not at
once apparent as it ought to have been. Special training or a
peculiar type of mind was necessary for its interpretation. Ward
realised this, and issued a printed pamphlet explaining it! He
realised, too, that this procedure was unusual, as indeed it was:
nor should it have been necessary.

'The circumstances of a Painter attempting an explanation or
description of his own work is a novelty which may be considered
as demanding some apology. This picture is intended rather as
an appeal to the understanding rather than the sense . . .

'It is contended by some, that a Picture should be made up
only of such materials as are capable of telling its own story; such
confinement would shut out the human mind from a depth of
pursuit in every branch of art. Poetry requires prose fully to
explain its meaning, and create an interest . . . The Argument of
Milton and Homer . . .

'I am not ambitious to be considered an Author, or if I had that
ambition, could I ever hope for success, for reasons which it
would be improper to intrude upon the world. [An unusual burst
of modesty]. I shall attempt in my simple style, an explanation
of my ideas as they occured to me.

'Let no one suppose this Picture to be undertaken in admiration of a spirit of warfare. War is to be considered as a preventa-
tive to mortification, the cure and restoration of a diseased
world.'

What is genius? asked Ward, and answered that it was a
powerful imagination regulated by a powerful understanding,
with an organic constitutional bias (physical or moral) to the
exercise of such power in a particular branch of art or science.

Shakespeare, he said, could never become a Garrick, nor Newton a Shakespeare.

'Men of genius were in three classes, those concerned with things as they ought to be and not as they are, potentates and powers who were of genius by the fact of being what they were, and a third rather minor grade. This was that multitudinous race of men with some distinguishing talent, who claimed the momentary attention of the world . . . are pitied and then die. They are ingenious men rather than men of genius. They are in their different degrees, frequently borne away by some eccentricity or enslaved by some propensity, by which they are kept to mediocrity.' Comment upon these remarks is super-fluous.

How extremely mistaken James Ward was in his observations of his fellow men is shown by his claim that temperance was one of the foremost amongst the virtues of his fellow countrymen, that Wellington was a clement man, and that the country was going to be more prosperous after victory than it was during the war, a pardonable mistake made by many people both then and later. 'Plenty in the steaming showers of Plenty', he wrote in ecstasy, 'profusely poured upon our highly favoured nation, to the filling of our barns our store houses and rick yards with an overflowing wealth.'

Nothing of this kind happened. By the early months of 1816 the Board of Agriculture was obliged to institute an enquiry into the state of farming and the distress of farmers. The grain that had been sold for years at famine prices was suddenly confronted with importations and prices dropped cataclysmically. Farmers were obliged to market their crops as soon as harvested. This flooded the market, so that prices dropped even lower. Farms were then thrown up by bankrupt tenants; notices to quit were given by others in the hope of the offer of reduced rents; others, still more desperate, simply drove off their livestock and carried their furniture away. Some others joined the pauperised labourers in their applications for parish relief. Wide areas simply dropped out of cultivation, especially in those districts where the high war prices had tempted people to grow corn on marginal or unremunerative land. Creditors everywhere pressed for their bills and great numbers of farmers suffered the humiliation of feeding the sheriff's officer in their kitchens. Landlords could not collect their rents; local tradesmen could not get their due. Tradesmen, shopkeepers, and, not the least important, country innkeepers suffered because the farmers had no money.

The immediate results of victory were severe hardship throughout the countryside. Bad seasons did nothing to help. Adjustment was slow, and was not complete for twenty years, when the last of several Parliamentary inquiries showed that, at length, things were on the mend. Landlords had to make great sacrifices of rent. The gloom of this depression helped reduce the demand for Ward's usual line of work. Landlords, who were fully occupied in reducing their expenditure and whose enthusiasm for improvements was quenched by falling prices, were not likely to breed livestock they wanted painted. If they did they naturally wanted the work done at lower prices. Ward was the last man in the world to realise this, and his attention was so absorbed in his *Allegory* that he had but little time for outside affairs. When he did consider these, as he did in the *General View of the Picture*, his conclusions were hopelessly wrong.

Nothing could so readily demonstrate that the colour of Ward's mind was becoming more darkly stained, than this pamphlet. *The General View of the Picture* issued in 1821 reads:—

The genius of Wellington on the Car of War supported by Britannia and attended by the Cardinal Virtues, commanding away the three demons, Anarchy, Rebellion and Discord with the Horrors of War.

Bellona, as the Fury of War, is urging on the horses with her scourge of many thongs while they are tightly held back by Humanity, or love to *mankind* seated upon the head of Britannia's Lion, while between these two contending principles, Bellona, or hatred to mankind, the origin of love to mankind, the winding up of the war. The horses are regulated by the Cardinal Virtues, Prudence, Fortitude, Temperance or Justice; Usurpation with the crown removed from its head and marked with blood, is

sinking under the feet of the horses. Opposition and Tumult
expiring under the wheels of the car, on the side of which are the
Rose, Thistle and Shamrock, England, Scotland and Ireland
which form the Car of War, and on its end is the Palm of Victory,
to which are endeavouring to fasten themselves the Passions,
Anger, Cruelty and Revenge, but who are overturned and sinking
under the feet of Charity, whose other foot is upon the emblems
of slavery, while she is raising her children into the bosom of
religion, who, risen above the clouds of Superstition, Folly and
Bigotry is pursued by the Harpies, Calummy, Malice and Derision
and bowing to the pressure of two monsters, Prejudice and
Obstinacy, who are immerging from the clouds of Ignorance and
Error, clinging to each other. Religion oppressed by these
enemies, stretches out her arms to Britannia for protection,
supported by Hope and led by Faith, who through the medium
of the Cross is directing her attention to the Deity immediately
under the glory of which is the Dove of Peace with the Olive
branch over the Angel of Divine Providence, which is expanding
its arms over the whole group, as taking the whole under its
regulation and under whose wings as its offspring, is Victory
ready to Crown the Hero, and Plenty with a full Cornucopia to
pour upon Britannia in the event of Peace, while a group of
children of various complexions, characters and sizes as the lesser
Victories are scattering the Roses of their Conquests over the
British Lion and the Genius of Britannia.

'In the background, expressive of the Allies, are Blucher and
Patoff in union with Wellington, bearing the colours of the
different nations engaged in the war; and in the front above, as
alluding to those principles which have disturbed the civilised
world is the Hydra headed monster falling from the clouds into
flame and confusion and remorse, under which are the monsters
Rapine and Fear, flying to Despair who is directing them into the
Abyss into which they are hurrying.

'From the dark clouds of Superstition and Folly and Bigotry
and under the immediate influence of Anger, Cruelty and
Revenge, Death is raising itself throwing off the veil as it sends
forth horrid and shapeless forms into the field, but which all

THE WATERLOO ALLEGORY FIASCO

sink into annihilation as they approach Humanity or Love to Mankind seated upon the head of Britannia's Lion.'

The explanation is nearly as tortuous as the picture. The thing had become an obsession, and Ward could think of little else. He did carry out a few other commissions in the intervals of this mistaken pre-occupation, and he did a little travelling. Perhaps it would be better to say that he took a little vacation now and then from the work that was to render him immortal.

The undertaking made him a poor man. He devoted much too much time to it. An artist's income depends upon the completed works he has delivered to his customers. Ward was obliged to get advances on the allegory, and engaged in acrimonious controversy with the British Institution about the possibility of the price being raised. He made rather offensive comparisons with the rewards gained by other painters of historical subjects, and stirred up a hornet's nest. His selection was condemned in the public prints by his rivals, and his proposed allegory received all the harsh criticism that jealousy dictated. He was contemptuously referred to as a cattle painter, and his claims to other consideration dismissed as those of a charlatan. The Institution was impressed, and its officials did all they could to impede the progress of the work by that system of stonewalling so well known and effective in the hands of all officials.

Then domestic calamity befell him. In the autumn of 1817 his favourite daughter Emma fell ill. She died after a painful illness during which the father paid her the most exhausting attention. Grundy, who appears to have had access to a diary I have not seen, records that the whole family required medical attention after her death. It took curious forms that threw a bright light upon contemporary medicine. Mrs. Ward's grief was assuaged by blood letting; George (the eldest boy, by then a practising miniature painter) had twelve leeches applied to his stomach; James himself was anointed with an ointment to produce an eruption which he naïvely hopes 'did him good'. Matilda (another daughter) is said to have been at the point of death for four days. She recovered, and a few months later married John Jackson R.A., a contemporary and neighbour, who had a daughter as old as her new stepmother. Ward approved of this marriage to a man of strongly marked religious principles despite the disparity of age. Two years later Mrs. Ward fell ill at the same season of the year, and, assisted by the practice of blood letting (twenty-six ounces of blood was drawn off), passed away in an aura of sanctity. This tragedy was followed by the death of the youngest son, Somerville, not much later.

Margate then seems to have been a favourite holiday resort with the artistic world. Ward and his wife went there in September, 1818, perhaps to recuperate from these manifold misfortunes, though whether any other members of the family travelled with them is not clear.

There was then great rivalry between the coach owners who carried passengers all over the country, and great competition for the trade. The business was complicated and required good powers of organisation as well as the outlay of a fair amount of capital. The average distance of a stage was ten or fifteen miles according to the gradients, road surface and quality of the horse-flesh. Each coach proprietor kept relays of four horses at every stage, and these stood harnessed ready to take the place of the exhausted team when it was time for the coach to arrive. Changes were made with a bustle of haste, noise, dust and apparent confusion. The coach was soon away again, the unfortunate passenger having to swallow a snatched drink and sandwich at his best speed; though some halts of twenty minutes or half an hour were made on a long journey so that the passengers could grab a meal. There were ten passengers if a coach was full; six were inside, and four shared the top with the driver, the guard and what luggage had overflowed the boot. The ordinary stage coach travelled from four to seven miles an hour, but the mails were carried at higher speeds up to ten or eleven miles an hour. These rates were quite exceptional. People who rode upon the mail coaches were great adventurers, both because there was grave danger of overturning in these comparatively lightly constructed and top-heavy vehicles, and because this tremendous rate of speed was believed dangerous to the balance of the brain. Stories were

Stallions fighting on a river bank

Fallen by the way

circulated in hushed whispers of persons who had arrived in London after a journey at such speed, only to perish of a resulting affection of the brain.

The fares on all coaches were high; Ward was still well enough off to afford them. Less well-to-do people travelled by waggons, those huge vehicles on their great wheels, six inches or more wide, hauled by eight or more horses. These waggons were used for the carriage of heavy goods about the country, and an amusing story of a journey in one of them is to be found in the eighteenth century picaresque novel. For short journeys the rural population went in the carrier's carts, that have been painted so lovingly by Gainsborough, Wilson, Lambert and Smith of Chichester.

The dangers and inconvenience of travel on the expensive stage and mail coaches were not mitigated by the vehicles. Passengers on the roof, exposed to all the storms of heaven, were only safeguarded by a low iron railway round the back and sides of the seats, and often had much ado to keep their balance. The modern controversy about opening or closing the windows was a constant source of squabbles between the 'insides'. And the coachmen were arrogant and drunken, tippling at every stage, and quarrelsome withall, as readers of George Borrow will remember.

The competition between the 'lines', too, led to other dangers that were fully appreciated by James Ward on his journey to Margate, and probably upon other journeys. No coachman could bear to be overtaken by another, a sentiment that is still general in these motoring days. The sounding of the horn by the guard of an overtaking coach was the signal for a desperate effort on the part of the driver of the one in front. Coach races on indifferent, often narrow roads were no less dangerous than the motor races of today on our much better roads. On the way from Ramsgate James Ward was very evidently quite terrified by a race between the coach that carried him, and another that tried to pass it to the imminent peril of all concerned. In his note of this journey he told himself that such high jinks ought to be put a stop to, though that would have been as impossible as it is today. In spite of all, the Wards arrived at Margate safely, as most people do still arrive at their proposed destinations.

E

Many people of his acquaintance were already there. Margate was the place to which Morland had retired in the 1780's, when he got rid of some difficult obligations. Since then it had been growing in popularity as a seaside resort. Nearly forty years later when Ward made this visit it was a place of growing importance, and was much frequented by the well-to-do. Ward met various people, either permanent residents or visitors. Amongst these was Fuseli and Mrs. Musgrave, Mrs. Pulteney and Mrs. Bellisares. Ansell was not at home when he called, but he had better fortune with Miss Rendall. He left some letters at a lodging for H. B. Chalon, a member of a family of well known, if not famous, painters, and Ward's much disliked brother-in-law.

Chalon was an animal painter, and a good one, though a man of uncommonly irregular life. He was anathema to James Ward on both counts. He was a formidable rival in the sort of painting that James excelled in, and he was not only unfaithful to Ward's sister, but he was drunken as well. Ward used all the force of his considerable influence to injure and impede Chalon. He told Lord Chesterfield that he was not fit to employ, and he continually disputed his right to be elected an Associate of the Royal Academy. This form of persecution he carried on even after Chalon's death, when he told Mr. Hall of the *Art Journal* that he ought not to mention Chalon without condemning his vices. It was a miserable business throughout, and shows Ward actuated by spite and venom. He delivered the letters at Chalon's lodging, and it is to be hoped they were pleasant to receive.

While at Margate Ward read *Guy Mannering* 'a tale full of truth and nature, full of innovation and originality', an opinion on which no comment need be made.

One expedition, made jointly with a Mr. and Mrs. Rich, was to Reculvers, where, as Douglas Jerrold wrote not so many years later, 'so goes the hoary legend – Pope Augustine impressed the first Christian foot upon the English shore, sent hither by good Pope Gregory . . .' and pretended to discern the exact spot. I gather that this was a sea trip and not too successful. The beef steaks provided were wretched, the accommodation poor, coupled with which was the discomfort of a contrary wind that caused them to beat off Birchington for hours. The agitation of the craft caused the usual agitation to novitiate seafarers. At length they had to cast anchor and await the tide. James was seasick till 2 a.m., and his wife ill with anxiety, a wretched business, not unlike some modern 'trips'.

The scene was pretty enough when they finally landed. 'How rich the swelling meadows', exclaimed Douglas Jerrold. 'How their green breasts heave with conceived fertility! And on this side cornfields; the grain stalk thick as a reed; the crop level and compact as a green bank. And here too is a field full of canary seed; of seed grown for London birds in London cages; the farmer shoots the sparrows – the little rustic scoundrels – that with felonious bill would carry away the grain sown for, made sacred to, Portman Square canary.' And indeed the whole district was one of the most intensively farmed in the whole of England, though hard times had fallen upon it, and some of the farmers were finding it difficult to keep their heads above water.

Ward spent some time painting Reculver Church, the grave-yard of which was already attacked by the sea. The graves were broken open and the ancient bones of the dead scattered, some of them being gathered by metropolitan visitors who carried back these gruesome relics to adorn their drawing rooms. Birchington was a pretty village and church; St. Peters a neat village with a charity school as a poor house, adorned with a picture of a fine group of charity apprentices painted by Bacon, if Ward's crabbed writing is not misleading. The people of the town knew nothing about it – a lesson, remarked this hardened moralist, in the folly of vanity, a lesson he might have done well to learn himself. The old Minster had become a large farmhouse and very little of the Monastery was left, though there was a very good clean village.

When they returned to Ramsgate the contrast was so great that Ward compared it to going to Portland Place from St. Giles, though of course the contrast was much smaller in scale. The cottages of a country village, though they might well be huddled together and dilapidated – at that time when labourers were on

starvation subsistence and farmers and landlords had no money
to spend on cottage repairs – could not have formed a rookery of
the squalid poverty and crime that lurked in the purlieus of
St. Giles. The village might house misery enough, the cottage
homes were doubtless small compared with the Augustan buildings of the new resort, but that is the full measure of the contrast
that Ward saw in so much more marked relief.

Whether Ward's aesthetic judgement was permanently
affected by his absorption in the *Allegory*, or whether it was
never of the highest, he made a false cast in this year by etching
a picture of Benjamin West's that had been painted in West's
nonage. When he saw the etching West told Ward that the picture was a jejune affair done when he was only eighteen, and
not worthy of the praise Ward had given it. It was a rustic piece,
and West had only done three or four others of trees in Windsor
Forest.

This may have been an attempt to do something to bring in
some ready money. Ward had always complained of being hard
up, and if his complaints were to be accepted at their face value,
his large income, amounting almost to great wealth, would still
have been the poverty of Thames Street. So the aspirations and
ideas grow; but the truth was that he was spending too much time
on the *Allegory* and the times were bad, so people were not prepared to pay the large charges that had formerly seemed reasonable to them.

The *Allegory*, too, hung fire because Ward was unable to
secure sittings from the Duke of Wellington for the main figure.
James believed that Wellington purposely avoided him, because
he was not a recognised portrait painter. Whether this was so or
not cannot now be determined, but Ward, stimulated as always
by opposition, though that may have been only a figment of his
over-fertile imagination, proceeded to demonstrate that his ability
was great enough to compass this branch of his profession as well
as those in which his merits were already recognised. He persuaded the Rev. Dr. Busfield to sit to him, bribing him with the
prospect of a free portrait. To pay himself for the job Ward engraved this portrait, hoping to gain a goodly sum from the sale

of the prints. This scheme was excellent, but was defeated by the departure of the Duke to foreign parts. The number of copies sold is not on record, so it is not even known whether James fully reimbursed himself for this enterprise.

Whether he was willing to sit for the *Allegory* or not, the absence of the Duke was an insuperable obstacle to the completion of the picture. James had spent the advances on the fee so he was forced to drop the *Allegory*, and do other work for the time being. He must have been miserable enough in Newman Street, now lonely and haunted by ghosts of his lost ones, wife, daughter, and son.

He sought refuge in the country. The Duke of Northumberland engaged him to paint some of his cattle, in particular, a *Persian Horse* and the *Lambton Hunt*, later engraved by Charles Turner for Mr. R. Lambton. While on this visit Ward called on Thomas Bewick, the great engraver of beasts, birds and fishes who lived at Newcastle-on-Tyne. Bewick was then about seventy, and to Ward, who was no weakling himself, looked remarkably strong. He had a keen hazel eye that was once as strong as a hawk's; now it was weaker he could not work so long as he used. Bewick was not thought to be rich, though a very worthy industrious man. James commiseratingly remarked that Bewick knew nothing of business, a defect he was well qualified to recognise.

Bewick was just such another type as Ward himself, one of those odd characters that developed in that markedly individual age. He held the most extraordinary ideas of personal hygiene. When in his youth he went to Newcastle to work, he always went home at the weekend. 'On setting out upon my weekly flights up the Tyne (from Newcastle to Cherryburn) I never looked out to see whether it was a good day or a bad one', he recorded in his *Memoirs*; 'the worst that ever fell from the skies never deterred me from undertaking my journey. On setting out I always waded through the first pool I met with and had sometimes the river to wade through at the end. I never changed my clothes, however they might be soaked with wet, or stiffened by the frost, on my returning home at night till I went to bed. I had inured myself to this hardship by always sleeping with my windows open (itself significantly remarkable in that stuffy age) by which a through air, as well as the snow, rolled down in a blanket, upon a mattress as hard as I could make it. Notwithstanding this mode of treating myself, I never had any ailment even in the shape of a cold while I continued to live in this way nor did I experience any difference until, when I married, I was obliged to alter my plans, to live and behave like other folk.'

Life in so remote a part of the country had always been wild and free but harsh, especially for the labourers and colliers. Bewick, the son of a well-to-do farmer and mine owner, had the greatest sympathy with the workers, particularly with those who strove to improve themselves. This was occasionally possible if one of them settled on a bit of the wild commons that everywhere abounded in the north when Bewick was a young man. Here, he said, poor men could find grazing for a few sheep, a Kyloe cow, perhaps a flock of geese, and mostly a stock of beehives. Squatting on these commons was allowed, or at least not prevented as it was in the south. One of Bewick's father's colliers gained for himself a great reputation for industry, sobriety and honesty. He lived in one of the lodges of the estate, 'and a garth besides was taken off the common for his use. For these he often expressed himself so highly pleased that he used to say that he was happier than a Prince.' There were many such squatters. Bewick admired them. They had little intercourse with the world and were truly original. Their only reading was the Bible, local histories and old ballads, and the isolation in which they spent their days was a stimulus to the exaggerated personal idiosyncracy of character, always so strongly marked in such people.

The local Lairds who lived upon and farmed their own lands ought to have enjoyed every earthly pleasure with good health, but they were a roystering, prideful lot. Many of them, having consumed their inheritance by their misdirected pride and folly, were driven into the towns to get a living. A prototype of the best of these was the famous sportsman, Squire Osbaldistone. Sporting Lairds like him did not farm in a very spirited manner but every farmer, however orthodox and traditional in his methods, benefited by the high war prices. A woeful change came about after the peace.

More inspired agriculturalists took advantage of the inflated war prices to undertake large schemes of land reclamation. Northumberland was one of the counties most susceptible to the process, and fortunate in being the birthplace of John Grey of Dilston, one of the most enterprising and skilful farmers of the time. He was born in 1785, left his name in the records of his county, and his mark on the face of his native land. 'When his father first settled in Glendale', wrote Lord Ernle some years ago, 'the plain was a forest of wild broom. He took his axe and, like a backwoodsman, cleared a space on which to begin his farming operations. The country was then wholly unenclosed, without roads or signposts. Cattle were lost for days in the broom forests. The inhabitants were as wild as their home – the Cheviot herdsman ferocious and sullen, the rural population uneducated, ill clothed and barbarous.' But the character of the soil was attractive to skill and industry. Men of the same stamp as Grey, or the Culleys, settled in the fertile vales, and by their spirited farming transformed them into cultivated districts, like the rich valley of the Till, once a wilderness of underwood.

Such men were not to be overwhelmed by the fall in prices and the disastrous after-the-war years. As Bewick said, 'Societies for the promotion and premiums for the encouragement of various desiderata blazed forth over a great part of the kingdom. Cattle, sheep, horses and swine, all of which were called livestock, occupied a good deal of attention, and in the improvement of the various breeds agriculturalists succeeded to a certain extent, and in some cases perhaps to a great extent. And yet I cannot help thinking that they often suffered their whimsies to overshoot the mark, and in many instances to lead them on to the ridiculous.'

He has a good word to say for his friends Messrs. Bailey and Culley, whom he, in common with all his world, recognised as amongst the foremost cattle breeders of the day.

Being an artist Bewick was often placed in a quandary when asked to draw portraits of the various improved animals. He was, for example, asked to make drawings of cattle and sheep to be engraved for the *General View of the Agriculture of the County of Durham* then being prepared as one of the series issued by the Board of Agriculture. After he had made drawings of the fat sheep he saw that they were not approved. There was at the time a 'rage' for fat cattle, and the beasts were fed to as great a weight and bulk as possible, 'but this was not enough,' complains Bewick, 'they were to be figured monstrously fat before the owners of them could be pleased. Painters were found who were quite subservient to this guidance and nothing else would satisfy. Many of these paintings will mark the time and by the exaggerated production of the artists serve to be laughed at when the folly and self-interested motives which gave birth to them are done away.' It is curious that amongst all the anathema to be found in Ward's papers nothing is heard of this complaint, but the paintings of which Bewick was writing certainly give rise to some such suspicion. His general good sense confirms it.

Ward did not complain of being asked to produce pictures of cattle larger than life because the conditions of the Boydell contract called for portraits drawn to scale, like Garrard's models. Ward's paintings may be taken as accurate representations of the beasts he saw and measured, though his cattle all have very fine necks.

It was not when on this visit to the Duke of Northumberland, and when he saw Bewick, that he painted cattle. His patron the Duke was a collector of recondite types of horses, and it was their portraits that he wanted. In this undertaking James was successful to a quite unusual degree.

Early in 1820 he had a bitter letter from his old friend Thomas Levett, whose father had died without leaving anything to his children. For some not very explicit reason this made it necessary for Thomas to raise £420. The father had left the whole of his property to his brother. Father lived to be ninety-two years in the world, complained Levett, was never known to do a good action, and left it with a heart full of envy, hatred and malice and all uncharitableness. Can such a man be saved? he enquired of his friend, whose opinion on the point was doubtless informed with authority.

Six months later Ward was at Ashbourne whence he went to

Derby and on to Wichnor Park. The weather was very variable. It was so hot one night at Ashbourne that he had to take the unprecedented step of opening the window and casting off his blankets. The next night it was so cold that he could not sleep although he had to share a bed with James, as travellers then so often had to do. Not only the weather but the times were 'fearful', and dark shadows of calamity surrounded him. Mrs. Ward of Mickleover was dying; Mr. John Ellams the same. Levett was cutting down a wood against his inclination in an attempt to meet his liabilities, and so far four men had been killed doing it. This was a life of tears and misery.

One pleasant thing that partly redeemed it was a gift Levett made Ward. It was a horse fourteen hands high. There was also some sport. Once in helping Levett to get rid of the rabbits on his estate, James killed eleven out of thirteen shots, a performance of which he was justly proud.

Though all at Wichnor was peace and harmony, James did not quite know what to think about keeping a horse as the circumstances of the time appeared to him very alarming. They were. A Select Committee of the House of Commons was even then sitting to discuss what could be done to alleviate the distress in agriculture, a problem they found insoluble.

Ward's taste for the old, the macabre, the pseudo, a taste shared by so many of his contemporaries, led him to an interest in an absorbing fad of the day. Amongst the things he asked George to send him at Wichnor, where he was busy painting many things amongst them *The Deer Stealers*, was a book by one Sheetzman, *A System of Craniology*, and a cast of the head with the bumps and lumps in it. The whole country was taken up with the pseudo-science of phrenology and had been for half a century. Its great propagator was George Combe, a Scotsman, Writer to the Signet at Edinburgh, who married one of Mrs. Siddons' daughters. He made enough out of his practice and his marriage to retire at the age of forty-five. He devoted the rest of his long life of seventy years to what he thought quite mistakenly were philosophical reflections, a credulity he induced no less than one hundred thousand persons to share, but then almost everybody wishes for wonders and for that reason is willing to accept esoteric mysteries.

In his youth Combe 'entered heartily into the then young science of phrenology with his accomplished brother Dr. Andrew Combe and a few other men of talent in the Northern capitals,' diffused a large amount of knowledge of the subject, and made it for some years a popular study. He published an essay based on the work of Dr. Spurzheim, to prove that man was merely a part of nature, an irrefragable contention. Man depended on the conditions of his original constitution and his subsequent nurture and education, for the character he was to bear through life, a contention few would quarrel with in these days, and his harmonious action with the other parts of nature surrounding him would secure his secular happiness. Combe sold one hundred thousand copies of his essay in this country, a percentage of the whole population that would be equal to the enviable number of five million today. He sold nearly as many in America and Germany; so his theories were well received amongst populations wishing for signs and wonders. It is no wonder that James Ward in his endless search for the springs of human happiness, a state that he could never realise, was fascinated by the subject.

Belief in the value of this science continued, and it is not, I think, completely exploded today. Then it was so firmly held that 'it certainly as a hazel rod, between the fingers of a gifted individual, discovers precious metals and waters beneath the earth, so certainly a phrenological adept by a discriminating touch of the nodosities on the surface of the head, detects the secret sources or springs of human action'. Gall and Spurzheim changed the name from phrenology to craniology when they asserted that they had determined the relation between the outside of the head with its internal organisation, a possible but unlikely relation. Combe wrote his essay, de Ville made phrenological casts, and George Cruikshank issued from his home at Myddleton Terrace, Pentonville, his *Phrenological Illustrations* in 1826. It was impossible that James should escape from this enthusiasm. His correspondence does not disclose the results of his reading in the subject. It is mentioned only in the request for the book.

The weather continued bad all through the summer while Ward remained at Wichnor. In August the wind from the Peak was cold and violent. It was so fierce that it turned over a waggon-load of hay with two men who were lucky enough to escape with bruises. Wichnor was comparatively low and warm and felt to James as if he were in a room with a fire, a characteristic exaggeration. He made several excursions while with the Levetts. He went to Lichfield Cathedral twice, and called on Mrs. Arkland, the Dean's daughter, to see her paintings. In telling George about this he refers to Chantrey's monument of the two children. He made himself popular with the clergy and received three invitations to dinner, accepting a fourth from one of Mr. Levett's relatives. He was so contented at Wichnor that he wanted to find an R.A. to take his visitorship in the painting school so as to avoid the necessity for coming up to Town for October and then setting out again. He heard that friends were staying at Leamington, and thought he would ride over to see them. The journey was only three hours' ride, and Warwick Castle was a fine object to see. Whether he did so or not is an open question. He asked George whether Sir Thomas Lawrence had finished his picture for the spring exhibition.

Ward was as happy as it was his nature to be during this summer. Matilda, his daughter and the wife of John Jackson, told him so. She looked forward to meeting quite a gay young gentleman on his return. For herself she was quite free from earthly anxiety in their little cottage at Lee, and having had toothache 'had plucked up courage to have the offending member plucked out.' She had been busy on the excellent job of making wine.

When he got back to London James found that there was a possibility of renting Hayden's studio – at a price. His own was not large enough to allow him to finish the *Allegory*. Hayden's was. The gigantic picture could be hung there and completed, provided the Duke would sit for his portrait as the centre piece. The snag was that the Wilsons, the landlords, wanted £1,000 for the lease and a rent of £100 a year. Our ancestors had nothing to learn from us in the matter of key money. James ought to have been able to find that amount without any difficulty if he had taken care of only part of his massive earnings of previous years. He had not, and his only recourse was the assistance of his long-suffering friends.

In October, 1820, James was at Portsmouth – for what purpose does not appear. From that place he wrote to his son George saying that Mr. Levett had promised to lend him £500 for an unlimited time upon proper security. Mr. Strachen would lend him £200, and he felt sure that Mr. Morant would make up the remainder. George was to close with Mr. Wilson, and to agree to pay an annuity of £100 a year to Mrs. Wilson for the duration of her life, provided the title was clear and Mr. Papworth, a famous contemporary architect, was satisfied with the state of the premises. He was to have the option of engaging Mrs. Wilson for a wage of £50 a year to superintend the exhibition of the *Allegory* when it was finished.

These complex borrowings and arrangements were brought to a successful conclusion, and the Duke, having consented at last to sit, the *Allegory* was completed with Ward's usual dispatch. No later than April, 1821, he wrote to the Duke of York asking him to inspect the painting. This ardent man had spent a good part of five or six years painting a picture that was nearly double the size ordered, and almost impossible to hang in any ordinary room, even in an institution like Chelsea Hospital. It was conceived in a mode that was long outworn. To most contemporaries it was quite incomprehensible without Ward's odd descriptive pamphlet, and it deified the Duke of Wellington, who, reverenced as he had been at the end of the wars, was regarded now with scorn and hatred by the public. Nothing of the kind could have been a success in the face of such obstacles. The *Allegory* was a major disaster. When it was exhibited for public inspection in 'Mr. Bullock's large room in the Egyptian Hall, Piccadilly', critics came to mock and the public to jeer. So few people offered their names as subscribers to the proposed engraving that it had to be abandoned, and this method of Ward reimbursing himself for the great expense incurred vanished.

When the painting was taken to Chelsea Hospital it proved, as

James might have expected, too large for the wall on which it was to be hung. The only thing to do was to double it down. Naturally this idea was abhorrent to James. He saw it as another part of the universal conspiracy to undervalue the work, and reduce his reputation. As an alternative he suggested that the gallery, being too small for the picture, should be pulled down and rebuilt with a wall large enough to allow the picture to be hung upon it. This was rather unreasonable, and the Council of the British Institution would not agree, much to James' astonishment. The cost would have been some £15,000. This they thought with some justice overmuch expenditure to incur for a building in which to house a picture worth £1,000. In the end all came to nothing. Ward's labour of years, under what he regarded as privations and mental anguish sufficient to make the strongest head or heart tremble, was treated with contempt, spoiled and finally handed back to his family. They are said to have cut it up into several fragments, all of which have vanished from the face of the earth.

By June of 1821 James had left his disappointment behind him, and set off on his travels again. He wrote with some animation to George – he always wrote to George – from Mapperton House, near Beaminster, on the 9th, telling an escape story that had come to his notice. This may be called the affair of Sturt and his dog. Sturt was a prisoner-of-war in France and bribed an American ship captain to take him home. Unfortunately head winds forced the ship to put back to port. Sturt was forced to hide in a sea-chest with his dog while the gens d'armes sat on it regaling themselves on the captain's liquors. The dog sensed danger, and was quiet though it was usually restless. Sturt later died and willed that he should be buried at Brownsea Island with his dog, but the executors put him in the churchyard. James makes the mysterious statement that he lost £118 by the business.

Mrs. Daw, with whom he was staying (?), had a Sunday School and the chapel adjoined the house in the old style, 'and which is the Queen Elizabeth style of building'. Was this Mrs. Daw any relation to the Dr. Daw, Ward's quondam partner, who apparently went afterwards to India? She may have been.

James found lovely country about Beaminster. It still is today, and always was. It was the one-time home of the Rev. George Herbert, the well-known seventeenth-century clerical poet, author of *A Priest to the Temple* and many other poems now all too infrequently read. James once again, like so many other metropolitans, looked to a country retreat from all the disappointments and distractions of urban life. 'If I had a humble cottage in a corner of it', he wrote, 'I should be well and negatively happy. More than that is not for mortals – certainly not for me.' He wrote again from Briseton Deverill advising George to make any sacrifice rather than create an enemy, advice that he would have been sensible to adopt as his own procedure. Complaints were still being made that James' prices were too high. Doubtless these complaints were justified.

Instead of accepting the conditions of a general economic depression, and reducing his prices to meet them, James thought it would be undignified to accept lower fees than he had been in the habit of charging when the country gentry were flourishing in the sunshine of war prices. He compared himself to George Stubbs and his prices to those Stubbs' pictures fetched. Today this looks like a ridiculous attitude and indeed it meant that James did not accept the change in the times and the relative decline in the value of money – if the depression can be stated in this way.

His great friend, Mrs. Eleanor Allnutt, tried to persuade him to act differently, but without success. During his widowerhood she looked after his shirts, neckcloths and shirt frills, sending them to Newman Street from her home at Clapham. She sat for a miniature to his son George in 1821.

Ward was in a great state of depression while in West Dorset. The delights of the country faded, and the smoke of London was like a cell in Newgate. 'My eyes are confused and seeing double. My head is in a constant stupor and my heart is made of lead and dragging me down.' The wretched sceptics, amongst whom it had been his fate to be cast, were responsible, and his sons did nothing to assuage the bitterness of his lot. They must beware of the snakes that hissed against them.

James found the Daw's home a haven in which all was health, harmony, love and peace, a little paradise. He was forced to leave it on a following Monday, but did not expect to reach London till Thursday. When he arrived he must again launch into the confused miseries of London tumult, 'but calamity he found everywhere as well here as in other countries'.

A month later he was still in the West Country, the state of his mind unchanged. He visited Stourhead and was greatly taken with the landscape gardening there. It is sufficiently impressive. It was all that could be wanted in the best modern style of nostalgic country loving, though all the trees had been cut down for money.

James professed to be sorry that Chalon was so miserable about the R.A., but was convinced that nothing could be done for him. He saw to it himself. 'A little while, a very little, and those in and those out of the Academy will sleep together in peace and yet we cannot help thirsting for happiness in this world and by it increase our misery,' he piously added. He said he was going to Weymouth. This watering place had become the fashion since George III made a habit of visiting it, and a White Horse had been cut in the hillside in the king's honour. It still figures there if I am not mistaken.

Nothing that James did at this time would prosper, though he went on painting with all his customary industry. He evidently sought a government clerkship for George, but failed to secure it – another grievance against the snakes in the grass, and the glib, oily tongues of the devils that pursued him.

Miss Allnutt tried to console him. She offered to let him a gallery in Pall Mall. She had visited the one he had got from Hayden several times. She begged him to bestir himself to make a recovery from his depression of spirits. She gave him just the religious consolation he required, assuring him that thousands of unseen angels attended his path. One of them was Eleanor Allnutt herself, a thing that James did not entirely appeciate.

All this depression of spirits may have been relieved when Ward was approached by the Americans, Thomas Sully and J. Earle. They wanted to arrange an exhibition of pictures collected

in England in a gallery established three years before at Philadelphia. Amongst the paintings they wished to include Ward's
Horse and Boa Serpent. The terms offered were not ungenerous.
The Americans undertook to pay half the cost of shipment and
insurance, and the profits were to be shared in the same proportion. The pictures exhibited were to be sold after the termination
of the show. This looked promising. The pictures were shipped,
but misfortune completed the deal. As already related the vessel
sank at sea, and was lost with all its cargo. Ward does not record
whether he received any payment out of the insurance or not.
The *Boa* picture of which he was so proud remains to us only in a
sketch that was later bought by the Marquis of Stafford. It was
still hanging in one of the bedroom corridors at Trentham less
than fifty years ago.

Ward's industry did not flag despite his jaundiced outlook. He
painted the large picture now known as *Regent's Park*, but first
called *Protection* and afterwards *Cattle with Landscape*. Once
again he set out on his travels in the autumn of 1822 to make
portraits of some of Mr. Arbuthnot's livestock at Thrapston, in
Northamptonshire. As an economic measure he travelled on the
outside of the coach though it was mid-October.

While at Thrapston he drew the bull *Romulus*, then the *Bull
and Cowman* and the cow *Maria*, as well as making sketches of a
grey horse and another of a spaniel with the horse. He found it
severe wear and tear to get one portrait done in a day, but he
managed to make some excursions as well though he only stayed
a week.

He visited the Duke of Dorset's seat at Drayton. The house was
magnificent but he could find no good pictures. Some fine – he
said the finest – Hereford cattle adorned the grounds. He listened
to gossip about Lady Althorp, who had paid a great sum of money
for a charm by which to have children. She had her wish 'a dead
born child and death to herself in the birth' – 'how careful should
we be to avoid presumption. God give me pardon and protection,'
wrote the pious but rather callous James.

He was equally callous about Henry Chalon's death. He called
it a blessed one. He could not forget that Chalon had once, many

years before, said that Ward could paint rustic horses well enough, but could not portray bloodstock, a job at which Chalon was then making a living. James carried his resentment beyond Chalon's grave, a quite unnecessary emotion as he had long been successfully painting bloodstock when Chalon died.

It had been planned to have the Thrapston pictures lithographed. James intended that his son George should do this work. George had so far had rather a chequered career. He learned mezzotinting from Samuel Reynolds, who in turn had learned his art from John Raphael Smith. Reynolds, 1773–1835, was an engraver and an adequate teacher, but James found an opportunity of quarrelling with him and ending George's apprenticeship. He called him a rogue. He may have been but, like Ward, he was a quick worker and used 'etching to strengthen the mezzotint' with success. He made engravings of many of Northcote's works, after Morland, and portraits after Reynolds. He was employed by Turner on his *Liber Studiorum* and enjoyed the patronage of Samuel Whitbread from early life. He was engaged as Drawing Master to the royal princesses and through them was offered many posts at court, all of which he declined, even knighthood. Many of his oil- and water-colour landscapes, shown at the Royal Academy and the British Institution, went to France and Germany. He is comparatively little known here. Besides being an original and powerful painter of landscape, Samuel Reynolds was a skilful landscape gardener and laid out the grounds at Southall and Mount Edgecomb. His son began life as private secretary to Samuel Whitbread, and for some years practised as a portrait painter. It was by no means his fault that George Raphael Ward suffered when his father cast away the remunerative substance of painting animal portraits and rural life for the shadows of allegorical work. James' own misguided ambition was the cause.

Many people felt sorry for James. Sir Thomas Lawrence showed practical sympathy for the son by employing him to make miniatures of his paintings. This work provided George with a sufficient livelihood until the death of his patron. James wished him to lithograph the portraits of Mr. Arbuthnot's animals, but

George was fully occupied. His father was forced to do this work himself, something quite new to him. It proved an attractive and practical novelty. In a couple of years James produced a set of fourteen lithographs from his own portraits of celebrated horses, and some others which sold well.

And suddenly the sullen sky of James' fortune took on a rosier hue. The year 1823 opened successfully with the exhibition of *Protection* at the British Institution, and a visit to Newmarket to paint racehorses at the behest of Mr. John Knight.

The undertaking was a mixture of success and failure. Ward got a good many introductions while at the famous racing centre. He breakfasted with Mr. Tattersall where he met General G. Grosvenor, brother to Lord Grosvenor. He began on *Sultan* on Thursday, on *Angus* on Friday. On the Sunday he went both to chapel and church, and walked to Cheveley House where he examined two of Ben Marshall's pictures. The following Wednesday he began a commission to paint the Duke of York's horse *Moses*. The picture was to be a companion piece to Marshall's *Ranker* at York.

Mr. Rodgers, a bookseller in the town, lent Ward a painting room, and showed him a horse and dog by Marshall for which he was asking twenty-five guineas. James did not like Dubost's Newmarket horses, done in France. He thought them 'as bad as maybe'. On Friday he began *Salem* and walked in Mr. Witherby's grounds to see his hunter and his Suffolk Punch. The following Thursday he returned to London. It was a lightning visit in the best style of Ward's excursions, but was, as usual, remarkably productive in the short time of the visit.

Throughout the year Ward was going to one place after another to work at a variety of commissions. In August he was again at Levett's at Wichnor. While there he dined with the Corporation at Lichfield. The weather and the harvest were surprisingly fine to the great joy of the farmers, who certainly deserved a piece of good fortune. George, that man of all work, was exhorted to visit his grandmother for whom James never lost his affection. James wrote again in September saying that he was to go to Sir Thomas Mostyn's in Wales to paint horses, and

that he expected to arrive there at the end of the following
month. At that time he intended to return to Levett's, and was
astonished to find that he was without money, something that
was perhaps a result of extravagance, but most likely merely
bad management. He asked George to send dressing gown, skates
and lacing boots as he expected to winter in the country. Stones
for lithography he ordered to be sent by the van instead of by
the canal, provided no very great additional expense would be
incurred.

This is the first and only time that Ward mentions canals,
and then only because he was giving instructions. He was as im-
pervious to this development of transport as he was to other
circumstances that did not immediately affect him. Only when he
had to make a choice between the slow water transport of the
canal, and the slightly less slow road transport does he think of
it. Yet the canals that had followed one another in rapid succession after the Duke of Bridgewater built the first between
Worsley and Manchester a few years before Ward was born,
had played a large part in the development of the economic
resources of the nation and so Napoleon's defeat. Between the
building of the first and the building of the last canal, in or about
1834, were seventy-five years of great prosperity for inland water
transport. The railways superseded them very largely, although
a few are still used. Others slumber in the quiet countryside, old
barges lying on their empty beds rotting away, like the locks
and other works that cost so much labour to erect, but are now
being restored to use for holiday cruises.

It is not so very surprising that Ward said nothing about canals
because they did not normally carry passengers: it is more than
surprising that he said nothing about roads, except to make an
extraordinary claim to have preceded McAdam in his ideas about
road-making. Such a large part of James' life was spent on the
roads that some comment upon their condition might have been
expected. There is none. Yet during his lifetime very great
strides were made in road-making, partly under the influence of
the turnpike trusts.

The first of these trusts had been established three years after

Charles II returned, and a century before Ward was born. The idea was that road users should pay for the maintenance of the roads by tolls charged for passage along them. A century later many of the roads were in a terrible condition as Arthur Young observed. By 1823 when Ward had at least thirty years' experience, there were over a thousand turnpike trusts controlling, not always very efficiently, some twenty thousand miles of roads. But as bad as some of the turnpikes were, the lanes and side roads which led away from them were no better than they had ever been. They were only dirt tracks, often very ill-defined.

The demands of the canal traffic made matters worse instead of better. Goods had to be carried to the shipping point and that concentrated traffic on what were formerly by-roads or lanes. Then came the road makers, local like Blind Jack of Knaresborough, national like Telford and McAdam. It was unfortunate that just as canals and roads were being made suitable for carrying heavy traffic the invention of the railway engine by Stephenson, and its trial run in 1829, should have superseded, or almost superseded, them. Both canals and roads fell gradually and temporarily into decay. Much of James' travelling in the 1820's must have been comparatively easy to him compared with his experience of thirty years before, especially in Wales, in the remote North and South-West.

Some time during this year James paid his second visit to the King at Windsor. This must have been between his trip to Newmarket and going to Wichnor. This bid fair for him. The King was delighted with his pictures of the royal horses. With His Majesty's consent James sent home for more pictures to show him. Some argument arose over the way in which one of the horses was depicted and, kinglike himself in his own realm, Ward ventured to dispute the matter with His Majesty. He talked at such length that the King was fain to declare himself satisfied and to call enough. This may have been why the King was too busy to see James when he brought the finished painting for him to inspect.

After he left Windsor James spent a couple of months with Sir

John Leicester at Tabley, near Knutsford, though it may have been that he was there only at intervals. While there he was asked to do a portrait of Sir John on a grey charger in the uniform of the Colonel of the Cheshire Yeomanry. The dangers of travel were impressed upon him when he was detained for three days in December at a wretched place called Baggilt, owing to gales, and finally crossed the Ferry in an open boat much overloaded with persons and baggage. On this voyage he thought he would be relieved of all his labours and woes. He was to have gone round by the steam boat but the wind was too boisterous. However he reached Knutsford safely and, I think, stayed there for Christmas.

The history of the next few years is a series of misfortunes and disasters. James still maintained his footman with a silver band upon his hat despite his burden of responsibilities and debts. He slaved away, continually complaining of his lot. It was none too easy, but he made it worse by his quarrels and bickerings with everybody, including his devoted son, George Raphael, who spent his life as helot to his father.

It was during this period that the pure comedy of the blacking factory happened; but though comic enough to read, it was just another disaster for James. London was the harbour of many émigrés from the French Revolution, some of whom did not return to their homes when the wars were over. Doubtless they were reduced to all sorts of artifices to earn a living. It is almost equally certain that there were native rogues who adopted this guise in order to engage sympathy and to dull suspicion of their grotesque projects. One of these, genuine or pretended, 'a reduced foreign nobleman' had invented a shoe polish, a profitable commodity in those days of horse traffic on muddy roads and of highly polished Hessians, if it could be successfully marketed.

Unfortunately the polish of the reduced nobleman was not stable enough. In wet weather it became liquid, and could hardly be distinguished from the mud of the roads. The idea fascinated James. After all it was a kind of pigment. What if he could make a waterproof polish! There was a fortune in the idea, or so he fondly believed. George was ravished from his engraving to become manager of a blacking factory, or rather to become a blacking factory. James was quite sure he had invented a water-proof polish. It had the power of restoring dried and perished leather, and was so firm that tissue paper bags treated with it held for weeks, or so he said. There was one thing lacking: it was the black colouring.

George made up a lot of it, and it was sold to the trade. It was a complete failure. No more orders could be secured for the water-proof varnish for black boots that contained no black. James was as furious as he was about the *Allegory*. Of course it was all George's fault that the blacking was not a commercial success and its failure only added to the financial embroglio. An idiot's failure that might easily have been a success in other hands. George indeed tried to introduce a black pigment into his father's for-mula and only called down upon himself Jovian thunders for doing so. All he did was to provide a good excuse for blaming him for the failure of the enterprise. It was another unjust blow from the misguided fates.

George, the ever devoted, willingly received the vials of his father's wrath. James Claude deserved them. He was another thorn in the father's flesh, having inherited his cleverness, but not the stocky stability that forced the father continually to strive against the misfortunes he brought upon himself, and the enmities of his own creation.

James Claude was quite unstable. He could stick to nothing, was a gambler, a rake and a spendthrift, doing nothing to help himself or to ease his father's stormy life. James got him a job with the East India Company, but in less than a year he was home again. James got him a job in the Tower and James Claude spent money lavishly wherein he followed his father's bad example. He was forbidden his father's house, and took refuge with his sister, Matilda, who was living quietly and happily with her elderly spouse; but after vagaries of a most stupid sort James Claude enlisted to escape his difficulties. He was again sent to India with his regiment, and was by all accounts a good enough soldier.

Matilda was living a humdrum life, but was contented enough, though in other circumstances felt she could have been a lady of fashion, something her beauty and talents certainly made possible. With her husband James had another of his incomprehensible quarrels. He could not let it rest, even when Jackson was on his death bed. The result was a long estrangement between father and daughter.

In those days any respectable unmarried man in difficulties looked out for an heiress to marry. The contemporary novel is full of this device; it forms a major factor in most plots. James Ward could not escape the habit of his age. His second wife was a Miss Fritsche of Leamington whom he believed to be wealthy. Unhappily the monetary fortune she was to bring was illusory. She brought James personal devotion and duty, and they lived happily together, but the marriage did nothing to restore his finances. The date of this marriage is not very clear, but from his correspondence it appears that the happy pair made a honeymoon tour in Wales during 1827.

Wales had long been a happy hunting ground for the numerous late eighteenth- and early nineteenth-century tourists, who travelled the country in search of the picturesque. A couple of years before his wedding tour Ward was in Wales. He wrote to George from the Beaufort Arms, Crickhowell, complaining that it was wet beyond living memory, though he had been sea bathing (he does not say where) with good results upon his health. He asked for the picture of the fasting woman and of the horses to be sent to him there.

Ward visited Merthyr Tydfil on this journey. He found everything concerned with the Ironworks most inexpressibly sublime and awful; but sublime and awful as the works appeared to his artist's eye all was not well with them. It was ten years since the war had ended their vast prosperity; ten years since rioting had broken out among the workers who had been reduced to destitution by unemployment, or to the verge of starvation by a lowering of wages, when the military were called in to restore order. Since then two periods of stagnation had menaced the iron and steel industry of the country. From the end of 1815 to about 1816 and during 1820, 1821, and 1822, much the same years during which farming had been in the lowest trough of depression. Ward remarked that Merthyr, like all other things, had fallen to the lowest ebb in 1825, and that one proprietor was losing above a thousand a year, who formerly kept one thousand to fifteen hundred horses at work about those mines. In the same year the price of wheat somewhat recovered, though it did not reach the high price of 1817 that had given a temporary fillip to farming. By 1822 it had fallen to less than half this, 44/7d., and, though it rose to 68/6d. in 1825, it fell again to 39/4d. in 1835, thus making the situation of the farmers and landowners highly uncertain.

The portrait of the Duke of York's racehorse *Moses* that James went to Newmarket to paint was shown at the Royal Academy in 1825. King George's *Soothsayer* had been exhibited in the previous year. A hackney, *Monitor*, belonging to the King was also shown in 1825. Both *Moses* and *Monitor* were engraved, and ought to have paid James handsomely; but whatever income he made was absorbed in the responsibilities that he never shirked, and the extravagance that he might well have avoided.

These horses were not by any means the first that James had successfully portrayed, and he continued to do this work. In 1826 he showed a portrait of the *Norfolk Phenomenon*, a Hackney that was taken to Yorkshire by Mr. Robert Ramsdale, and played a large part in improving the breed there and in other parts of the north.

Grundy states that Ward went to Paris in the winter of 1825, and was there received 'by the French authorities with distinguished courtesy'. A large copy of a Georgione in the Louvre had been commissioned in advance, and the élite of the English visitors gathered round his easel daily. Among these was the Duke of Bedford, to whom Ward was already known. The Duke gave the artist a commission to paint a picture for him to add to the paintings at Woburn.

James' funds ran out in Paris, and he had to wait there until rescued by a remittance from George. After he got back to England the subject for the Duke's picture, which had been left undecided, began to be discussed. Amongst Ward's papers is a letter from the Duke that deserves quotation because it throws

some light upon the way in which subjects were chosen. Dated
from Paris it runs:

Dear Sir,
    I have to acknowledge receipt of your letter of the 27th which
I found at Paris on my return from Nancy yesterday. I like both
the subjects you have suggested for your picture, but I think
I should prefer the first viz; 'the Drayhorses drawing a Butt of
Beer . . .' as admitting of more variety and perhaps being more
nationally characteristic than the other. The subject however is
not absolutely new as Mr. Garrard many years ago painted a
picture of Drayhorses in a Cart at Mr. Whitebread's Brewery at
Chiswell St., which is not in Mr. Whitebread's collection (it was
engraved by William Ward) and although I do not admire
Mr. Garrard as a painter as much as I do as a modeller of animals
yet this is his best picture. I have no fear however of your treating the subject infinitely better and making a much grander
work of it! I have said this. I will leave it to your own feeling and
discretion to select which of the subjects you like best. The
English Drayhorse is unquestionably an animal of very grand
character and such as is seen in no other country; perhaps you
might heighten the contrast by placing a traveller and pony in
some other part of the picture, particularly as the scene is proposed in a country village. The Duchess requests me to thank
you for a letter she has received from you mentioning a sketch
you had sent her which however is not yet come to hand.
                                                        Bedford

    Besides this commission Lady Agnes Buller wrote to Ward
early in 1826 inviting him to do a picture of an Italian greyhound
for his constant patron the Duke of Northumberland. The
Examiner, too, was kind to him, saying on 14th May 'Mr. Cooper's
Battle of Zutphen is inferior in its execution and colour to its
general composition and character especially opposed to the
contiguous Rubenesque Battle near Boston by J. Ward R.A. in
which the dazzling light pervading it adds greater intensity to the
admirable furor of the numerous combatants.' But he was just as
short of money as ever, and so was George. James, once again at
Wichnor, sent George £5 saying that God alone knew when he

would get any more. He had expected a loan of £100 from Fritsche, his future father-in-law, but he, too, was in the same boat.

Ward was not the only artist of the time who had a grievance. His friend J. Bacon was another. Ward had visited him in his country retreat at Sidmouth six years before, and in 1826 received from him a long letter in which Bacon called himself a broken-down artist and expressed the deepest sympathy with Ward's disgraceful treatment.

Bacon's own story of his life in this letter is comparable with some phases of Ward's own, though Bacon did not suffer under Ward's temperamental handicaps. Bacon began his career by giving some tests of talent, a phase that is difficult to understand. At thirteen years of age he was admitted as a student to both the plastic and life school of the Royal Academy, but he failed to secure the silver medal, something he attributed to prejudice. The next year he did even better. He was awarded the gold medal, but was not made a member because a rival, whose work was not so good as his, invited the Committee to his house. Bacon scorned to work his selection that way. His work was much praised, but he did not get Nelson's monument because Northcote wished Flaxman to have it, nor Pitt's in the Abbey because of Pitt's friends. The allocation of these jobs did not, he declared, depend upon talent or study, but on the capricious influence of pride and ignorance and self-conceit, actuating a phalanx composed of those infallible beings called gentlemen.

This somewhat impertinent history of himself helped him to sympathise with Ward. His rivals were all making large fortunes, but he had been forced to retire to Sidmouth where it was cheaper to live than in London, sixty-five pounds there being equal to one hundred in the metropolis. Meat in general was only 7d. a pound, except veal that could be had for 5d. or 6d. Poultry generally was 2/6d. or 3/- a couple, and bread was then 9d. a quartern loaf, a reduction of 25 per cent. Servant's wages, too, were low. These were the advantages of living in a tiny village on the coast of Devon, not yet the seaside resort it became later. Bacon was well aware that he dare not hope for so great an acquisition as Ward's co-residence in the neighbourhood. Ward would have found it impossible to settle so far away from the centre of things despite his passion for travelling. Bacon's story, when every allowance is made for his own bias, shows clearly the jealousy between artists, and severe, rather unscrupulous, competition between them.

Though he was fifty-eight and spent a lengthy honeymoon tour in Wales during 1827, James had no scruple in telling George that he was young and could wait to get married. George was by that time approaching middle age. This advice was contained in a letter dated from Tenby, the extreme point of the happy couple's planned tour, a most romantic spot. This tour cost James nearly a hundred pounds, rather an extravagance in a man who always declared himself so penurious, but a forgivable extravagance.

During these years James Claude the son was persistent in his demands for assistance. He always promised that each request for help would be the last. Living at Grove End gave him an additional walk to work and caused him to wear out many boots although he had them very thick and nailed. This was a specious and probably imaginative plea. Again he had only one coat during one year, another filial complaint that was not very original, even if true. Such piteous claims have always been used to touch parents' hearts and open their pockets. These are specimens. There is a mass of such letters amongst James Ward's correspondence. James replied that there were men in the city supporting a wife and family on a pound a week, but he did not fail to give James Claude most of what he asked for, which wiser people might have thought rather foolish.

Sometime, perhaps after his marriage, James had acquired a tumbledown cottage at Cheshunt at a rental of £40 a year. James Claude was the cause of his immediate retirement there. He had been made bankrupt under the name of James Ward of Newman Street. This did his father no service. The old man determined to go down to the country to live.

Before he did so he tried to retrieve his fortunes by putting up a collection of his works for sale at Christie's, stating on the title page of his catalogue his determination to retire to the country. The paintings included the *Group of Cattle in a Landscape* of the natural size painted in emulation of the famous picture of the *Bull* by Paul Potter in the Museum at Amsterdam; various portraits of horses and animals of distinguished beauty or peculiar breeds; subjects from domestic life and allegory; particularly the sketch for the Waterloo painting then hanging in the hall at Chelsea College; a whole length portrait of the Duke of Wellington and a copy of the Marquis of Stafford's *Bath of Diana*. It was a symposium of all Ward's works. One hundred and five paintings were set out in the catalogue, but the sale was disappointing. Sales realised £1254.9.6d. of which James received £992.13.6d. George bought in to the value of £79.5.6d., and Christie's to the much larger amount of £514.4.6d. *A Sportsman and his Gamekeepers* reached the highest price noted in James' catalogue, £300. The Waterloo *Allegory* sketch and another picture £200 a piece; the *Wapeti or North American Deer*, £150; but other prices were relatively low, and a good many portraits of horses were among the unsold lots.

In the latter part of the year Ward was once again at Crickhowell demanding the engravings and letterpress about the fasting woman, whose feats he had apparently not yet realised were tricks to obtain notoriety and money.

He wrote to Lord Londonderry in June, 1830, saying that the picture of *Charles*, a horse, was nearly finished. He was almost ready to do another *Arabian* instead of the picture of *Walton*, the celebrated racehorse belonging to Sir John Shelley, Bart., that had been sold for £120 at Christie's in the previous year. He had let most of the Newman Street premises though he kept a few rooms there, and was even then under the operation of moving to the country. At Roundcroft he made his headquarters for the rest of his long life that still had nearly thirty years to run.

The Boa Serpent

James Ward as an
old man

James Ward

The Triumph of
Wellington

CHAPTER VII

Old Age at Roundcroft

Just before he left London something happened that should have
been a warning to Ward. It should have told him plainly that the
times were not good for luxury trades like his. A portrait of the
Duke of Wellington 'with a Hydra', a study for the *Allegory*, had
been sold at Christie's for £200 to a purchaser whose signature is
no clearer than any other signature. The name looks like
Holsworthy. He lived at Brookfield, Hathersage, Sheffield, and he
wrote to Ward asking for the delivery of the picture so that he
could show Ward's 'lovely work' to 'the great folks who will be
down on the 12 August'. With this request he warned the artist
that 'us poor agriculturalists' were in poor case. Consequently
James must not expect payment until this buyer visited London
in the following summer.

The state of agriculture was indeed deplorable. It had not yet
recovered from the disastrous effects of the wartime expansion of
the arable and the great decline and unstable fluctuations in
prices ever since. Rents had been reduced 50 per cent or more
from the war-time level, but this did not enable farmers to keep
their heads above water. The sudden and unpredictable changes in
prices made farming more of a speculation than it always was.
Attempts to meet them by growing more or less wheat failed
dismally, and the well meant efforts of government to regulate
the market by a sliding scale of import and export duties only
made confusion thrice confounded. The seasons were bad. Wet
prevented the clay farmers from working the land, and from
manuring it and some deserted their farms which fell into ruin.
Then sheep rot broke out in 1830–31 and the sheep died by the
million.

F

Farmers facing such difficulties could neither pay rent nor
wages. Consequently landlords had to cut down their conspicuous expenditure, including things like pictures by Ward and
his competitors. Labourers without employment or with minute
wages were faced with starvation. The artisans in the new towns
thought their distress due to improved machinery and broke out
into riots, the Luddites burning and destroying the mills, that
were at once their tyrants and the source of their living. The
rural labourers took a cue from them and, seeing their winter
employment in threshing by the flail beginning to vanish as
threshing machines were introduced, went about the countryside
destroying machines and burning ricks which was no way to
increase the supply of bread. In the riots of 1830–31 when
'Swing' and his proselytes were at work, agrarian fires blazed
from Dorsetshire to Lincoln. The riots were suppressed with the
greatest severity, but these events did nothing to amend the
situation.

The Royal Academy exhibition of 1830 contained a delightful
portrait of the artist's mother in her eighty-first year, a lovely
thing, but Ward's reputation gained nothing from *The Fall of
Phaeton*, *Venus rising from her couch*, nor *Diana at her bath
disturbed by Acteon*. Two animal pictures, *A Maltese Ass and
Foal* and a *Spanish Ass and Foal* were in his natural style. This
was an elaborate collection; the following year he only showed
a self-portrait, perhaps because of the upset consequent upon his
move from London, or it may have been because he decided to
develop his suddenly self-recognised talents as a writer. Nobody
else could recognise them.

James' brother-in-law Fritsche tried to dissuade Ward from the
unhappy pursuit of writing versical descriptions of his pictures.
He told him that these descriptions lowered the value of the
picture one hundred per cent, and added in no uncertain terms
'don't let the public read such damned doggerel stuff'. One
example of this immortal song is sufficient. It was written on
hearing a lady remark, 'This fine morning makes me want to
live a little longer.'

What is this? Desponding Spirit
Why, Not thou absorbed in night?
Tho' all's sin, in Christ is merit;
Tho' all's dark, in Christ is light.

Why in light, then go I darkling?
Wandering drer in gloom to stray,
The Daystar, ris'n, brightly sparkling
Calls; I go, yet wish to stay.

Stay why? in a world so madly
Rankling deep, in anxious thought
Aspiring high! now drooping sadly,
Soul! with contradictions frought.

Besides poetry Ward indulged himself in the horrors of religious controversy with a pamphlet I have read but failed to understand. It had the title *New Trials of the Spirits, in reply to two Sermons preached by the Rev. Henry Blunt, M.A., written in a letter to a friend by James Ward R.A.* It was followed by two other pamphlets. One was *A Defence of the Beard* which he read to his long suffering colleagues at the Academy in a beardless age, perhaps in the hope of starting a new fashion. He had himself grown a beard, after he made the self-portrait exhibited in 1831. The other was on *The folly of docking horses tails.* I have not been able to find remaining copies of these anywhere, but perhaps that is no loss.

The retreat to Roundcroft was enlivened by one happy incident. James found a devoted servant in a disabled gamekeeper from Norfolk whose name was Pay. This man had been wounded and permanently crippled in an affray with poachers. Such affrays, battles to the death, were by no means uncommon between bands of poachers and gamekeepers at that time.

The game laws were incredibly severe like all other criminal legislation. Before 1800 punishment was by a few months in prison, but a second conviction was punished by whipping and a year in gaol. The punishments were awarded by the injured parties, the landowners, who were the Justices, and not likely to be unduly lenient. These were the persons entitled to kill game.

Landowners who possessed a freehold estate of at least £100 a
year, or leasehold of £150, or the son and heir apparent of an
esquire or of parents of higher degree. An Act of 1800 prohibited
all other persons with a stronger deterrent than ever. Any two or
more persons found in any forest, chace, park, wood, or almost
any other place in the countryside carrying nets or guns or any
other apparatus for taking game, could be seized by keepers or
servants, and haled before a J.P. often the owner of the land and
the game, who was empowered to treat them as rogues and
vagabonds. In 1816 it was made possible without any debate at all
to transport a convicted unarmed poacher for seven years; this
punishment was reduced next year and only inflicted on poachers
carrying arms.

Two causes combined to increase poaching; 'With the growth
of upper class riches and luxury there came over shooting a change
corresponding with the change that turned hunting into a
magnificent and extravagant spectacle. The habit set in of preserving game in great masses, of organising the battue, of main-
taining armies of keepers. In many parts of the country pheasants
were now introduced for the first time. Whereas game had
hitherto kept something of the wildness and vagrancy of careless
freedom of nature, the woods were now packed with tame and
docile birds, whose gay feathers sparked among the trees before
the eyes of the half-starved labourers breaking stones on the
road at half a crown a week.'

The labourers were indeed in a parlous state. They were the
most hard hit of all the rural classes. There was little work and
their miserable wages were subsidised by the Poor Rates under
the system adopted by the Speenhamland magistrates in 1795.
The unemployed were set to work breaking stones on the road at
6d. a day and that wage was supplemented by a bread allowance.
The men were sent round to all the farms to seek work and from
this came to be known as Roundsmen. All were so poorly paid
that some outdoor relief had to be given them. The diatribes of
William Cobbett were rather more than justified. The men were
so desperate. Cobbett tells a story that bears the imprint of truth.
A young man was asked how he lived by breaking stones on the

roadside for half a crown a week. He replied that he did not live upon it. He poached. 'It is better to be hanged than starve to death,' he said. This was the penalty for resisting arrest by presenting a gun or attempting to stab or cut a keeper, or other such person. There was a good deal of change in the Game Laws and the punishments were slightly varied from time to time but remained excessive. Lord Brougham in 1828 strongly condemned the tribunals before whom the cases were brought. They were not worse than the Turkish Cadi, and, though in his opinion the magistrates were not likely to be corrupt, they were strongly influenced by the infringement of their privileges and property that poaching represented. One in seven of all the criminal convictions in the country between 1827 and 1830 were for poaching, and the number of persons found guilty was 8,502, many of whom were not eighteen years of age.

Not all the dissuasive legislation with its scandalously cruel punishments; not all the spring guns and mantraps that were so freely used; not all the strong forces of armed keepers could keep starving men from taking game. Some of it they ate; some of it they sold, though before 1828 it was illegal to sell game. In some places the business of poaching was organised, and the game was sent to London by the stage coaches, most likely by the service of the inn keeper. Some men indulged the practice because it was dangerous sport and offered adventure to the crafty woodsman. In the result affrays between poachers and keepers often ended in maiming and death. It was one of these battles that provided James Ward with a servant devoted to his master until the death of the man separated them, though the religious feelings that they shared must have given them a very present hope of meeting once more in the shades of a future life.

Roundcroft was rather dilapidated, and James had frequent disputes with his landlord about repairs, but he must have found living there pleasant. He had secured a good servant in the man, Pay, and he bought an old pony and phaeton for a trifle. In this he and his wife ambled round the countryside, then perfectly rural, whenever he felt inclined to take a few hours of leisure from his interminable painting and sketching.

His lithographic work enjoyed some dubious popularity with no profit to himself. He complained to George that pirated editions were being sold all over the country for a couple of shillings apiece. These may have been of the twelve famous horses Ward did for Akerman. There was no remedy, but this popularity brought no grist to the mill. George himself was in difficulties. He could not get hold of a commission. His father, himself very reluctant to reduce his own charges, told George that his prices were too high. They may have been. James added that if George and James Claude would only devote themselves to the business side of their father's affairs they might easily make £500 a year for themselves, besides a thousand for their devoted sire. This was optimistic, but he was ready to back his unfailing hope of still larger successes by the most unremitting labour.

Farming had not yet recovered from the disastrous effects of wartime effort and peace time re-adjustments. Consequently the landowners, the leaders of the landed interest, were striving by all possible means to bring back prosperity to the industry. All over the country groups of landlords and tenants, of owner-occupiers and so on, had formed themselves into societies that held meetings where problems could be discussed. By co-operative, not individual effort shows were held on a smaller scale, but after the pattern, of Woburn and Holkham sheep shearings. At these shows prizes were awarded for the best animals of local breed exhibited by their owners. In East Anglia there were, and indeed still are, several famous local breeds of animals. The Essex pig, the Suffolk Punch horse, Red Poll cows and Suffolk sheep, the Norfolk sheep, all these were well known throughout national farming circles, and the farmers who bred them were justifiably proud of them. This local patriotism led one of Ward's admirers and patrons to work out a subtle scheme for his advancement. It may be that T. Myers, Jun. who lived in Chapel Street, Paddington, then a very different place from what it is today, may have had some financial interest in the scheme, but whether this was so or not does not emerge from the correspondence. He may have been quite disinterested in his efforts on Ward's behalf. He certainly did not fail to encourage him in the most formidable terms. Myers' idea was that Ward should travel through Essex, Suffolk and Norfolk with introductions provided by him, and try to secure commissions for painting animals and rural scenes. His presence in the locality was to be an excuse for him to attend the annual dinner of the Suffolk Agricultural Association, where he might meet people who would want such work done without making too direct and obvious an approach.

The story of this effort remains in a series of hortative letters that Myers sent to Ward during the tour, and in a brief diary of the journey kept by James Claude. He went with his father as a companion and secretary, without very much enjoyment of either task, though he spent his time agreeably enough in shooting and dining with various people while his father was painting. Myers was unsparing in his advice and rather overwhelming in his demands for industry and determination to succeed on Ward's part. He even went so far as to suggest methods of painting to the artist.

On 24th August, 1833, Ward and his son rode to Thaxsted via Hoddesdon, Sawbridgeworth and Bishops Stortford. At Thaxsted they called upon the Rev. Mr. Gee, evidently the incumbent. They found Thaxsted church very ancient and beautiful, as so many other people have since. Thence they went to Sir W. Eustace and so on to Moynes Park, an Elizabethan-style mansion owned by Mr. Gent, whose collection of pictures was dismissed as complete daubs by James Claude in his diary. It is to be hoped that he was more tactful verbally. Here they were met by Mr. and Mrs. Thorpe of Chippenham near Newmarket. James received a pressing invitation to go there to paint a favourite racehorse and the three pretty daughters, a significant sequence of orders.

Myers had evolved a rather over-elaborate scheme for securing orders for Ward. Through Mr. Gee, Ward had been introduced to Lord Henneker, one of the members for East Suffolk, and a vice president of the Agricultural Association. One of Sir Thomas Grover's sons was a neighbouring clergyman and Mr. Gent and Myers thought a letter from him to Sir Thomas, another vice president, and M.P. for Suffolk, would be useful. 'Measures had

been taken' to ensure that some of the principle members of the
Association should propose that portraits of the 'Chief Prize
Animals' every year should be painted and exhibited at the
British Institution or the Royal Academy the following spring
and summer. These pictures should be raffled for at the price
paid to the artist to avoid expense to the Association. Myers was
confident that this would be a popular scheme. Many people
would take tickets on the chance of getting a valuable and
interesting picture for a trifle.

Though the local Agricultural Association was promoted by
the landowners and well-to-do tenants it could not then have
financed this project out of its funds. Both Suffolk and Norfolk
were counties where the four course rotation had been adopted
soon after it was introduced and this rotation was wheat, turnips,
barley, clover in each of the successive four years. Of these crops
wheat and barley were for sale and the turnips and clover were
grown for feeding sheep and cattle on the farm to produce meat,
butter, cheese and wool, as well as other by-products of the
animal-breeding industry.

In the very year that Ward went to these counties to attempt
to revive interest in the luxury business of having animal
portraits made, Mr. Robert Wright, a Land Agent of Norwich
complained bitterly of the losses incurred in growing barley. He
came of farming stock and had been a farmer occupying 'never
less than 400a. and sometimes 600a.', areas that still constitute
a large farm, until he was thirty years of age. He had been
forced to sell a good deal of the 1832 crop at 22/- a quarter, a
price that was only equalled in the depression between World War
I and World War II. This was an example of the great difficulty
the farmers had to face; ruling prices were much lower than they
had been. If a man had sold off his live and dead stock in 1833
after farming for an eight years lease the prices realised would
have been much lower than when he started though 'the ex-
change value had not diminished compared with other things'.
Indeed the lower sum realised would have enabled the farmer
to stock another farm of the same size; so in effect he would have
been as well off though not nearly so much money would pass

through his hands. Consequently he would not have so much to employ in improvements or to spend on luxuries like paintings.

In the current circumstances of hard times for farmers and landowners, Myers' scheme had a good deal to commend it. The members of the East Suffolk Agricultural Association would get their prize animals painted and recorded by a famous artist, and they would incur no expense if the pictures were successfully raffled. Members too, had as good a chance as any other ticket buyer of getting a cheap picture. Last but not least, James Ward, if he secured the job, could be certain of remunerative employment for some years.

While the scheme was maturing Ward went to Great Yeldham on the Essex-Suffolk border, where there was a reputedly old picturesque oak that was a desirable subject for a painter of his stamp. It had been mentioned in the Court Rolls of the Manor some six hundred years before, according to a statement in the correspondence, and is still standing and carefully preserved.

Ward made sketches in pencil, but found it an unexpectedly difficult task though he was received with great civility by Mr. Mason of Old Oak Farm. While here the Wards stayed with Rev. Mr. Way, of whom James Claude approved as highly genteel and forming a perfect contrast to the Gents. They were also invited by Mr. Hilton of Sible Hedingham and Mr. Badham of Bulmer.

Mr. Mason wanted a portrait of a favourite horse, provided the price was not too high. This gave Myers an opportunity, that he did not fail to take, of adjuring Ward to adjust his prices according to the necessities of the time. Other people, too, in the neighbourhood wanted horse portraits. Painting them occupied the father, shooting and dining out the son, until 12th September. Then they went to Colchester and slept at the Castle Inn.

Next day they rose early and rode to Ipswich before breakfast. Myers had advised this, and supplied an introduction to Admiral Page, but when they called the Admiral was not at the address given. Myers had depended upon the Admiral to provide further introductions, and told Ward to get to Saxmundham on the 14th. Being disappointed of Admiral Page they went there on the 13th

and arrived at 3 pm. only to find that the annual dinner of the
East Suffolk Agricultural Association had taken place on the
previous day. After so much preparation and exhortation it was
unfortunate that some inexplicable confusion about the date of
the dinner should have led to Ward missing it.

Ward made two calls upon a Mr. King, a Surgeon of Saxmundham and a member of the Association. Nothing came of
this and on the second occasion King was in bed. James was however honoured by a call from Lord Stradbroke and went to
Aldeborough to call upon three other people with no result. He
then went to Campsèa Ash, but found Mr. Wilson absent on a
visit to his brother in Buckingham, a series of mis-haps that no
one could have foretold, but which did less than nothing to forward Myers' scheme. No sketch was made at Campsea Ash that
day, but a mill near Saxmundham was drawn. The following day
Ward painted 'a beautiful Ram and Ewe of the Norfolk breed',
the property of Mrs. Webber of Sudborne Hall. At Alderton he
made a water colour sketch of a prize Suffolk stallion belonging to
Mr. Plant.

While he was doing all this James received a very angry letter
from Myers explaining, what James must have known very well,
that it was unlucky that he had missed the dinner. Two people
had written because they could not find him there. He must get
in touch with Lord Stradbroke and Sir Thomas Gooch and do
various other things he had already done. Once again he is told
that he must reduce his prices. Few landed proprietors could
afford one third of what he habitually charged for his work.
A vicious stroke was added. Lord Western, that great Essex landowner, would be glad to see Mr. Ward at Felix Hall, though he
was employing both Landseer and Harvey. The former possessed
all of the social graces that were so lacking in James Ward. He
used them to the full in exploiting his talents, though Ruskin
later expressed the opinion that Landseer was inclined to empha-
sise the animals in his paintings and to depreciate the human
interest in their favour. This, of course, made him a more formidable rival to Ward than ever, especially as he was in the full
flower of his maturity, whereas James was becoming an old man.

Myers asked Lord Western to recommend Ward to Coke of Norfolk, who probably already knew something of him, and who was then becoming the doyen of English agriculture, but nothing seems to have resulted from this. Myers for his part was certain that he had omitted no means in his power to promote Mr. Ward's object, and hoped to see him when he returned home from Newmarket.

Soon after receipt of this letter James evidently decided that he had got all the data for future pictures that this journey could yield, but he could not resist the opportunity of going to see Capt. Manby, inventor of the lifeboat. The father and son started home on the 25th September, riding 57 miles in one day, a fine performance in a man of sixty-four whom Myers thought it necessary to exhort.

The results of the tour were disappointing. The very ingenious plan to find James a competence for the rest of his life was defeated by a series of those petty mischances which play so great a part in most people's lives.

The painting of the Yeldham Old Oak was completed, and exhibited at the Royal Academy in the following year, 1834. Ward made several other pictures and sketches, one of them was the Norfolk Ram and Ewe already mentioned. Myers was not satisfied with this picture. He thought that the Norfolk breed of sheep was coming into fashion so Ward should add a wether to complete it. He need not go back into the country for a specimen. A butcher of Bond Street, rejoicing in the appropriate name of Giblet would be able to supply one. This was a broad hint to Ward to stick to animal subjects if he wanted to add to his very great reputation. James must have been bitterly wounded by this suggestion. All his ambition was to flourish in some more elaborate and recondite style of painting.

Probably after seeing Myers in December, 1833, he wrote a petulant memorandum. 'I am too old to run about the country districts plying my works to innkeepers and farmers, who after all would be better pleased with the works of a Suffolk pot-house Cooper than a Ward. It is impossible for me to be running about the world as if seeking a reputation which is so well established and unalterably established. And after all this I am to be told nothing but my want of industry can prevent my want of Success.' Myers was less than just to Ward in his nagging exhortations to industry, but no more so than Ward to Cooper, to whom he applied such a scurrilous adjective.

Abraham Cooper, the cattle and animal painter, came from a tradesman's family just as Ward did. He was the son of a tobacconist in Red Lion Street, Holborn. Later his father became an innkeeper at Holloway. Abraham got a job at Astley's, the horse trainer and riding master, and, when he was only thirteen, began to draw horses. This talent he developed so that he was given the job of painting horses for Sir Henry Meuse of Ealing at the age of twenty-two. Sir Henry became his patron, and this may have been Ward's excuse for the epithet. Cooper was self-trained and studied art by copying the engravings that Ben Marshall made for the *Sporting Magazine*. He himself contributed portraits of many horses to the *New Sporting Magazine* and in a more elaborate vein painted the *Battle of Waterloo*, etc. He too enjoyed a long life and died at the age of eighty-one in a cottage to which he had retired at Greenwich. This career contains nothing that could justify Ward's venom, except a taste, common to and profitable for many artists of the day, for painting cattle and animals.

The tour to East Anglia and the failure of the scheme that dictated it, was a great disappointment to both Myers and Ward. It was the last attempt Ward made to secure continuous, if not permanent, employment. It bears remarkable resemblance to the Board of Agriculture – Boydell scheme of his youth. It was not any more satisfactory in the long run, but had similar results in getting Ward other jobs, and supplying him with material for future pictures.

The failure of this Indian Summer of James Ward did not cause him to abandon painting. Far from it. In the year of Queen Victoria's accession he recorded that he had hardly been out of his painting room for months. The results pleased him, and he continued to show at the Royal Academy for many years thereafter, but times were changing. The opening of the reign inaugurated nearly forty years of renewed prosperity for British farming, but the demand for James' work was not renewed.

He would not swallow this bitter pill, and attempted to solace himself with a long continued acrimonious correspondence with the British Institution about the treatment of the *Allegory*, and with the British Museum about that of the *Gordale Scar*. At the same time he tried to stimulate the British Institution to revive another premium scheme that had been dropped. This was to give £1,000 for a picture three feet high by four feet six inches wide depicting the success of the British Army in Spain, Portugal and France, rather a tall order. James secured a copy of the original conditions from William Barnard, the Keeper, and hoped the scheme might be instituted again. This was a forlorn hope, circumstances having changed so much, but James proclaimed it to be one of the arrangements of heaven that hope is the last thing that leaves us.

His reputation must have remained at a high rating; at least he was so well-considered that aspirants to fame thought it desirable to secure introductions to him. A Mr. Colman sought one through Mary Thorp of 4, Pritchard Street, Bristol. He had been an artist for many years and was coming to London in 1838 to study some more. He had seen Sir David Wilkie who had received him kindly. He was recommended to Ward as a very humble man who needed encouragement, a man of deep piety who would find a congenial companion in James.

James was now a man approaching seventy, but his industry did not flag; and the revival of agriculture gave him some grounds for hoping that his fortunes might be restored. The Academy Exhibition each year contained some of his work. Unfortunately he persisted in trying to establish himself with such fancies as *The Triumph of Sin, Death and Hell*, and *Love flying from Sensuality and Dissipation*. In other conditions he might have been persuaded to abandon this sort of subject, but the new ideals of the farming community did not lead to renewed demand for animal portraits.

The Board of Agriculture, which had been so keen on such things, became moribund in the depression after Waterloo, and when the Government decided no longer to finance it, expired of inanition, in 1822.

The great Arthur Young, too, and many others of its foremost supporters were dead. A new generation with different ideas looked to other means to secure the advancement of their industry. In place of the Board of Agriculture established with the Government's benediction and largely financed by government funds, the new generation, a generation of individualists, determined to start a private society of their own. This was first discussed in 1837. The English Agricultural Society was established in 1838, being incorporated by Royal Charter in 1840, when the Queen became a patron. The greatest of the nobility were founder members, no less than four royal dukes and two others of the Queen's cousins being numbered among them. Lord Althorp, now Earl Spencer, one of the last, was known to Ward, but the slogan of the new society, 'Practice with Science', shows how little their aims coincided with those of the artist. The Royal Agricultural Society of England set out as its objects, the collection of information likely to lead to practical benefit in the cultivation of the soil, to carry out experiments to that end either direct or by the co-operation of a practising farmer, to encourage men of science to improve implements, agricultural chemistry, the veterinary art and so on, but these objects were not of a kind that could be depicted by paint on canvas. The establishment of the Royal Agricultural Society was at once a sign of the revival of farming, and of the farmers' attention to methods of progress. The Society took the place of the Board of Agriculture as the official (but not government) body concerned with agriculture. It took an equal place with the Highland and Agricultural Society that had long represented Scottish agriculture in the same way, and supported and extended the more localised activities of the much older Bath and West of England Society.

Ward's interest in allegory secured him a job that he would not otherwise have obtained, that is if the vague references in the correspondence are not misleading. This was the design of a window for Hoxton Church portraying the baptism of Jesus; but

I have been unable to secure any final evidence about this. A hint about it is made by one A. E. Kelly, who wrote to Ward in November, 1839, suggesting some slight alteration in the design. He was then seventy years of age.

The last twenty years of his life passed in the doldrums, always on the verge of poverty and tainted by the disappointment and unhappiness that had always discoloured it. Nevertheless his habits of industry survived and he exhibited annually at the Royal Academy until 1855, but the prices he received for his pictures were comparatively small. Some that were included in an auction of the Royal Academy, G. Dawe's collection, only made about half of what Ward considered they were worth. The *Yarmouth Cart* made £6.10.0. The *Village Church* £12; *Disagreeable Company* £10; the portrait of *Haphazard* £20. Unfortunately Ward was only interested enough to make a note of what his own work fetched so the catalogue does not provide a basis for comparing these prices with those given for the other works sold then.

Things went steadily from bad to worse. Ward had definitely fallen out of fashion in a changing world. His exhibits in the Royal Academy were still numerous, but it is evident that the pictures did not sell, or if they did it was for prices that did not prove sufficient. By 1847 Ward was in very low water indeed and he was forced to apply to the Royal Academy for a pension. 'Finding now the infirmity of age rushing upon me', he wrote to John Prescott Knight, the Secretary, 'I wish whatever income I may have to last for life and put in such shape as to render it impossible that the whole should be wrung again from me. I wish to be enabled to continue my habit of industry (for the Royal Academy alone) with a free mind unshackled by tormenting contrarity of advice and abuse and to be in some degree raised above the awful state which has nearly plunged me into the situation of a Culprit brought before the Judge to receive sentance, for Life or Death, instead of uniting on conviviality with my Brother Members on the Annual Festival.' This was a pathetic frame of mind for a man of nearly eighty years of age who had in his day been supremely successful. He was granted a pension.

Some idea of the way in which Ward was living at Roundcroft
may be gathered from a proposal he made to George in that year
for letting the cottage at five guineas a week in order that he
might go to the sea for a while. The rent would include the
services of a man, the produce of his cow, garden stuff, the use
of the pony chaise – the pony always shied after a mile or two –
and eggs, the tenants to feed the poultry.

The gallery in London was let, and James was happy to be
able to shut himself up in his painting room, not out of the surrounding atmosphere, but out of the world. It was a world into
which he no longer fitted. The country was no longer pre-
dominantly agricultural as it had been when Ward was born, and
even when he was flourishing during the French Wars. It was
rapidly becoming industrial. Great new towns had been built in
the North across Yorkshire and Lancashire, almost from coast to
coast; a similar development had taken place on the North-east
coast and in the Black Country. Here were hungry mouths
aplenty, but the low prices corn was fetching just before Queen
Victoria came to the throne created in some minds the illusion
that food supply had overtaken population. This was incorrect.
The failure of the potato crop all over Europe in 1845, and the
disastrous harvest of that year quite clearly demonstrated that it
was an illusion. The farm labourers were in deplorable straits;
the town labourers little better. The rising body of wealthy and
influential manufacturers, led by Cobden, demanded the aboli-
tion of the Corn Laws, so that plentiful supplies of cheap food
might be imported from Europe and across the Atlantic to keep
their costs of production low. The famine of 1845, the hungry
forties, gave them precisely the lever they needed; more perhaps
than the long-continued efforts of the Anti-Corn Law League,
the 'rain rained away' the Corn Laws. In 1846 they were
stringently modified. Only a nominal duty of 1/- a quarter on
foreign corn was charged after February, 1849; this small tax
was abolished in 1869. The modification, and finally the repeal
of the Corn Duties did not immediately have the disastrous
effects that the landed interest anticipated. It did mark the
changing emphasis on the two phases of the national life, a

change that was to become more and more marked as the century progressed.

Evidence of this was the building of the Crystal Palace and the holding of the Great Exhibition in 1851. One of the most famous of Ward's pictures was honoured there in 1859. It was the *Bull Family* painted in an attempt to outdo Paul Potter, and first shown in 1821. This picture James either gave or lent, in anticipation of a testamentary bequest, to his son George Raphael, and it was shown at Manchester before going to the Crystal Palace. George eventually sold it to the nation for £1,500. He was not so successful with the Waterloo *Allegory*. The *Bull Family* had been praised highly by Sir William Ross. H. W. Pickersgill said it surpassed Potter's, and Landseer referred to its extra brilliancy. J. P. Knight esteemed the subject natural and the picture natural; in his opinion the painting ought to be in a national institution. All the animals were, he said, painted from originals in the grounds of Mr. Allnutt at Clapham. Unfortunately these praises did not sell the picture to James' advantage, and he blamed George for proposing to incur the expense of a frame for a time. Alas, he said, an old man of eighty cannot look forward to time.

Some complex and incomprehensible financial arrangement had meantime been made with a Thomas Griffiths 'in consideration of all the pictures, drawings, sketches or prints' then in Ward's possession at Newman Street. Whether James raised a mortgage or bill of sale on this property for £200 or whether Griffiths was to pay him an annuity of £200 a year cannot be decided from the surviving papers. The correspondence is extraordinarily difficult, and it is little wonder that Ward complained that he could not understand what was going on. Some parts indicate the one payment charge, and others suggest a permanent income. What, if anything, resulted from the negotiations cannot be discovered.

And so this great man's life drew towards its close. George Jones wrote to him in 1850 saying that his current subjects like Jones' own, were not much in vogue. If only Ward had some of his admirable horses and cattle they would sell; but that was dubious optimism. Ward was unable to attend the general meeting of the Royal Academy in 1851, 'because of his advanced years', though he greatly approved of Mulready's motion about varnishing. He thought Sir W. Beechey's whole length of the Queen of George III appeared to lack force as hung. It was altered and spoiled. Sir Thomas Lawrence's head of the Duke of Wellington had too much brass and silver when seen at Mr. Arbuthnot's in the country as compared with Sir Joshua Reynolds, Wilson's and other portraits. Another remark then made was that while Sir Joshua presided over the Royal Academy, Fuseli was a fine colourist, but when Reynolds died Fuseli degenerated. Ward once changed the tones in one of his pictures on varnishing day. Fuseli told him he was spoiling it. Ward altered it back. The real evil was the established practice of varnishing.

Though so old a man his correspondence shows no sign of any decay of his interest in his profession. It is naturally inclined to be garrulous as old age is said to be, and less naturally, to contain oddities like:

> In vain to paint, to preach or to write
> A pig, Sprite, Angel or Devil
> While man with his Soul hates the Light
> Because in his heart he loves Evil.

There was a remaining flicker of interest in his projected pictures. T. A. Prior wrote him in April, 1852, telling him that he was looking forward to seeing Ward's picture *Daniel in the Lion's Den* in the May show that year. Ward could not resist a dig at the Pre-Raphaelites who were becoming all the rage.

'Pre-Raphaelites Dialogue
between A and B   Absolute Blockheads

A. How highly are we privileged now! by living in the human intellects maturity. What a surprising man was Sir Isaac Newton, what wonderful things he brought to light.
B. Ah, but you are speaking of him when he was an old man!

What must he have been like when he was Six *Months* Old,
think of that? try to imitate what he was then, think of the
nourishment that is drawn in by the Pap-spoon.
A. Egad? Mr. Spooney, you are right. What warmth and comfort
there must have been in the Swaddling Bands?
B. Right! to be sure I am – come back to the vigour of Swaddling
Bands! – the world has now got old and crazy.'

In August James and his wife went wandering in Kent. They
travelled to London from Ramsgate on a Saturday 'in the first
class carriage in *three* hours for 10/- each. Surely this may be
called the march of Intellect'. It was certainly very different
from the time so long before when he was terrified by the racing
tactics of the drivers of mail coaches along the same route.
Nevertheless undertaking the adventure of travelling in one of
the primitive trains of those days was a sign of the dauntless
spirit of this courageous old man of eighty-three.

For some reason James made a list of Mrs. Ward's trinkets in
this year. It is not without interest as showing what a fairly well-
to-do woman of the mid-Victorian period was likely to possess in
that way. The list was 12 rings, 1 pearl clasp, 1 Ivory pin, 1
Acquamarine brooch, 1 pair Jet ear rings, 1 Coral brooch, 2 Cap
pins, 1 Pearl drop, 1 Elephant, 1 Ruby brooch, 1 Heart with hair,
1 Lapis Lazuli pin, 1 Cornelian brooch, 1 small Pear earring,
1 long ornamental pin, 1 Pearl brooch, 1 pair Pearl earrings,
1 Coral necklace, 1? brooch, 1 Jet cross, 2 Jet brooches, 1 black
necklace and cross, 1 carnelian necklace, 1 pair jet earrings,
1 gold chain.

Three years later in 1855 a paralytic stroke put an end to
Ward's painting. From then till his death in 1859 time marched
on placidly with him. His interest in theology was still vivid. He
comments strongly upon the annotations made to a copy of
Pilgrim's Progress that had been given to him. Since this was
one of the first books he had read time had gone full cycle.

The death of this almost forgotten nonagenarian roused once
again a small spate of enthusiasm and praise. 'He was an early
riser and indefatigable worker and continued to exhibit six or

eight pictures every season at the Royal Academy till his 86th year when an attack of paralysis stayed his hand. He was a man of gentle manners, amiable disposition [sic] and varied occupations. His piety was unaffected and profound.' In his later years his Bible was his constant solace. His second wife survived him.

His work is almost forgotten despite the fine examples in the national collections, but much against his will he was a master cattle painter, and though there are some all too frequently remarked upon flaws in his work, within his limits he is unsurpassed. His rural scenes too, have a gentleness often absent from the cattle paintings. They demonstrate another side of the nature of this man of character, a man significant of the great season through which his country and his compatriots passed during his long and serviceable life.

Bibliography

J. T. NETTLESHIP	*George Morland and the evolution from him of some later painters.* 1898. Other books about Morland are by: G. C. Williamson, 1904; G. Dawe, 1905; J. T. H. Bailey, 1906.
JULIA FRANKAU	*William Ward, A.R.A. James Ward, R.A. Their lives and works.* 1904. See also this author's *Life of John Raphael Smith.* 1902; and *18th century colour prints.* 1900.
C. REGINALD GRUNDY	*James Ward, R.A., his life and works, with a catalogue of his engravings and pictures.* 1909.
RANDALL DAVIES	*English society in the 18th century in contemporary art.* 1907.
E. S. ROSCOE	*The English scene in the 18th century.* 1912.
WITT BOWDEN	*Industrial society in England towards the end of the 18th century.* 1925.
W. GAUNT	*English rural life in the 18th century.* 1925.
C. REGINALD GRUNDY	*English art in the 18th century.* 1928.
A. E. RICHARDSON	*Georgian England. A survey of social life, trades industries and art from 1700 to 1800.* 1931.
A. S. TURBERVILLE	*English men and manners in the 18th century.* 1929.
R. H. MOTTRAM	*Old England illustrated by English paintings of the 18th and early 19th century.* 1937.

CHRISTOPHER   *The Picturesque. Studies in a point*
  HUSSEY   *of view.* 1927.
Idem.   *British country life in art.* 1937.
D. M. STUART   *Regency roundabout.* 1943.
FRANCIS D.   *Art and the Industrial Revolution.*
  KLINGENDER   1947.
NIMROD (CHARLES
  APPERLEY)   *The life of a sportsman.* 1948.
DENZIL BATCHELOR   *The Turf of old.* 1951.
AUBREY NOAKES   *The world of Henry Alken.* 1952.
ELIZABETH BURTON   *The Georgians at home, 1714–1830.*
                      1967.
R. W. HARRIS   *Romanticism and the social order,*
                      1780–1830. 1969.
STELLA MARGETSON   *Leisure and pleasure in the 19th*
                      century. 1969.
Idem.   *Leisure and pleasure in the 18th*
                      century. 1970.
FRANCIS SHEPPARD   *London 1808–1870. The infernal wen.*
                      1971.

This list could be almost indefinitely expanded by including the books about art, about individual artists, about social conditions, about the agricultural state of the country and the great improvers, the rise of an industrial society and so forth. The above are only a few of the books read in the process of preparing this book.

Index